Australia's Southwest and Our Future

AUSTRALIA'S SOUTHWEST
AND OUR FUTURE

Jan Taylor

SOUTH AUSTRALIA

Streaky Bay

Kangaroo Press

This book is dedicated to the memory of Simon, and to Anne, without whom I would never have been able to move into the realms of wildlife photography and writing. Had it not been for them I would probably still be a Civil Servant working on mammal pests in England.

million years ago

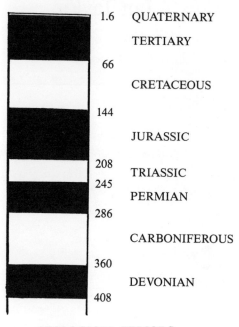

GEOLOGICAL PERIODS

First published in 1990 by Kangaroo Press Pty Ltd
3 Whitehall Road (P.O. Box 75) Kenthurst NSW 2156
Typeset by G.T. Setters Pty Limited
Printed in Singapore through Global Com Pte Ltd

ISBN 0 86417 350 4

Contents

	Preface	6
1	Kings Park and the Invaders	13
2	The Jarrah Forest under Siege	25
3	The Wheat-Belt: Total Land Clearance	40
4	The Goldfields: Pastoral Degradation	54
5	The Nullarbor: New Species, New Invaders	68
6	Archipelagos: Farming and Alga-Culture	82
7	The Fitzgerald River: Changing Climates and New Landscapes	96
8	The Stirlings: Atmosphere and Climate	109
9	The Karri Forest: The Changing Role of Forestry	122
10	Mammoth Cave: Rising Sea Levels	139
11	Coastal Plain: The Value of Diversity	148
12	Rottnest: Ecology and Human Society	160
	Index	174

Preface

Visitors coming from the French ship *Naturaliste* in 1801 saw a great number of pelicans when they entered the Swan River. These huge birds are still commonly seen there and are abundant at Mandurah.

Why are we trying to conserve native fauna and flora? The answer may seem obvious, but if one takes a longer term view, one has to admit that our efforts are merely putting off the inevitable mass extinctions by perhaps as little as a generation. The growths in modern technology, global population and affluence will inevitably destroy the last of the wild places, great mammals and natural ecosystems unless some radical change in direction occurs. We are in the middle of a mass extinction which will wipe out most of the animals and plants that have evolved since the dinosaurs died out 66 million years ago.

Over the past twenty years that I have lived in Australia I have travelled extensively in the Southwest, learning about its fascinating geology and living natural history. During this time I have become increasingly aware of the changes taking place and have been able to compare the rate of change in the relatively pristine environment of Western Australia with that of my native England, and places I have visited in Southeast Asia, Africa, and North and South America.

I have drawn this experience together in the book as a diary of observations and thoughts recorded as though during an excursion around the Southwest. I try to reveal through informed eyes the fascinating natural history of the area and the effects of modern mankind on the landscape and ecology. Inevitably my record leads to the conclusion above. This pessimistic view is becoming universally accepted by biologists, but I was very conscious in writing this book of the need to try and find answers and hope for the future. Our city-based society is likely to get tired of hearing about the negative aspects of human interaction with the environment unless there is positive direction as well.

I think there is an answer which does fit within our present economic framework, and it comes with exciting intellectual, financial and social benefits. I have developed this theme from the premise that we are still only a primitive society—our technological age having only been here for a single lifetime—not thousands or millions of years as one would expect for other intelligent societies in the Universe. The most severely damaging primitive feature comes from the fact that our society is still based on foundations which were laid during the Neolithic, when people first started clearing the forests, growing crops and tending domestic stock. Virtually all our agriculture and research is based on this Neolithic way of thinking and it pervades our management of the planet, as we continue to act as though land and resources were unlimited.

I have built on my suggestion mentioned in *Evolution in the Outback* that a new technology will come in the future. The principle is known to any ecology student: the nearer we get to the sources of primary production the greater the productivity. I believe future societies will base their primary production on algae and cyanobacteria because these organisms are the fastest producers. They can produce food at an incredible rate compared to wheat, and at an astronomical rate compared with beef or wool. We may not like the idea of eating algae, but it is now becoming clear that biotechnologists will be able to tap the enormous wealth of technology held within the existing species of the globe. With this technology it will become possible to use genetically engineered bacteria and fungi to manufacture from algae anything from beef protein and bread to paper, wool, plastics and building materials. This massive new industry would be most efficient in the lands which have been laid bare by human mismanagement—the arid regions of the world—and have tremendous spinoffs in terms of power generation, waste recycling and freshwater production. It could even put a value on greenhouse gases and reverse the current build up of carbon dioxide in the atmosphere. In time it would replace sheep and beef farming, even wheat, rice and the use of forest-cut wood. Biotechnologists can already make a cellulose paper, potential textiles from spiders' gossamer and plastics, all using genetically engineered bacteria.

I conclude that the answer to the question: "Why try to conserve native fauna and flora?" is therefore twofold. We need to preserve the natural ecology of the planet so that we can survive and appreciate the wonders of nature, but it also holds within its DNA the enormous technological wealth that could form the foundation of the future "Post-Neolithic" age— our future.

I believe the second answer could appeal to even the most hardened economists, industrialists, entrepreneurs and developers. Hopefully politicians will also gain popular support if they can divert at least some of the money earmarked for devastating weapons systems into this area of research. By doing so they would be helping to defend the global human population from impending disaster.

The natural history of the book is local, of course, but the message concerning the recent human impact on the environment can be seen anywhere. For this reason the reader may be able to find aspects relevant to all other regions of the globe.

I thank Dr Stephen Davies for sharing his extensive information on Eyre, Dr Barbara Main for information on the spider *Chasmocephalon neglectus* and Joanna and Don Box for many happy days at their property near Pemberton and for leading trips to the Yeagerup Dunes, Black Point and up the Murray River.

My thanks are extended to Professor C. A. Parker and Dr Arthur Weston for critically reading the manuscript. They made many useful suggestions, however I am entirely responsible for whatever errors, bald statements and omissions are present in the text. I also thank Naomi Segal for some cautionary words, and Dr Michael Borowitzka for guidance on my biotechnology reading.

The book could not have been written without Madeleine's unfailing support and breadwinning role. I thank her also for many hours spent improving syntax. I also thank Ross for printing the lettering for the map, Graham for letting me use his photograph of Major Mitchell cockatoos taken at Eyre and Jonathan and Graham for loaning me their rabbits, Hopalong and Ricochet immortalised in the drawing.

The inclusion of so many photographic illustrations in this edition which form such an important complement to the text, would not have been possible without the assistance of Anne Jones whose financial backing is most gratefully acknowledged.

Jan Taylor, April 1990

Over 500 Black Swans were seen at once in the Swan Estuary by Captain Stirling in March 1827 on the way up the river. No such aggregations are seen there today.

Red wattlebird on blackboy flower. Many flowers in Australia are designed to be pollinated by birds; insects visiting the flowers are merely robbing the plant of its nectar. This bird is a kind of honeyeater, feeding mainly on nectar and insects which visit flowers.

Climbing sundew. These plants festoon the Kings Park vegetation with their glistening leaves during springtime. The leaves catch flying insects, especially termites and midges, but many of the insects are eaten by sundew bugs which use the plant to catch prey for them.

View over Kings Park. The park was originally heavily wooded with jarrah and tuart trees. Most of the jarrahs were logged and old saw pits can be found in the park, while the tuarts are dying back from unknown causes. They may be dying through loss of shading from the original closed canopy, changes in water availability caused by the growth of a dense ground vegetation, or through increased insect activity as mentioned in the text.

Kangaroo joey amongst kangaroo-paws. Kings Park used to be a favourite hunting ground for the local Aborigines who used fire to flush kangaroos and wallabies towards men waiting with spears. The only native mammals remaining in the park are possums and bats, but rabbits, foxes, rats, mice and cats can now be found there.

South African gladioli in Kings Park. This area of bushland was preserved with the idea
that it should be kept to show succeeding generations what the countryside looked like
for the first European settlers. It has therefore had the longest period under European
influence and shows what is likely to happen in other forests and reserves in the future.
Most of the original trees have died and the ground vegetation is under threat from a
host of exotic plants.

1 Kings Park and the Invaders

When I first came to live in Western Australia in 1969 I was fortunate enough to work near Kings Park, and often walked through the bushland areas. Like so many visitors from overseas, I experienced a feeling of shock, because the environment was so different from any in the Northern Hemisphere. The only things I recognised were introduced weeds like scarlet pimpernel, sow-thistle and Canadian fleabane. Even the birds and animals were so strange that my eye was drawn to the familiar for reassurance: the rabbit burrows, fox droppings, and painted-lady butterflies. The first settlers must have experienced a similar but even more severe culture shock, because they did not even have the benefit of seeing some familiar weeds. The foundations of Kings Park were laid by Septimus Roe in 1831, but it was not gazetted as a Public Park until 1872. In 1890 John Forrest extended it to 400 ha, wishing to retain the area as native bushland to remind future generations of the countryside experienced by the first European settlers.

Seeing kangaroo-paws (*Anigozanthos manglesii*) reminded me of Ellen Mangles, Captain Stirling's wife, who came from near where I was brought up outside Guildford in England (the laboratory where I later worked on squirrels was also only about two kilometres from Woodbridge). She would have been brought up in the Surrey countryside, with its landscapes of green fields, hedgerows, winding lanes, downland, commons and woods. She would have wandered through meadows and under the soft green leaves of overhanging beeches and oaks and into coppices, where a musty smell would rise from the damp leaf litter, mouldering into a rich humus. It is hard to comprehend the heartbreaking wrench that many of the early settlers must have experienced, coming directly from rural England without any experience of life outside their home village let alone in other parts of the world. Many probably felt a deprivation akin to that felt by Aboriginal peoples for their recent past.

For most there was no going back to England, and it was incumbent on them to do something with the local landscape to survive. Their response was to remove local vegetation as swiftly as possible and try to re-create the green pastures of rural England. They supported moves to populate the countryside with memories of home — with rabbits, foxes, robins, blackbirds, larks, blackberries, goldfinches, deer, pheasants and many, many other species. "Acclimatisation Societies" were formed all over Australia, with the aim of importing mainly European species in an attempt to re-create the English rural flora and fauna. It became a cult to such an extent that everything seemed better than the natural Australian bush life; they even tried to create a wild menagerie with such animals as blackbuck from India, and eland and ostriches from Africa. Thankfully only relatively few of the species brought in became established, and most are still largely restricted to urban areas and farmland. However, increasing numbers are becoming "acclimatised" and are spreading into the bush with potentially devastating impact.

I suspect that some of this alien feeling about the Australian bush remains today, deeply ingrained in our society, because our art, literature and science are firmly based on this English-language, Anglo-Celtic cultural background. The Australian bush tends to be thought of as harsh and ugly, and I must admit that when I first came, most of the gum trees looked very staggy and deformed compared to the smooth outline of the broad-leaved forest I was used to. The trunks were blackened by fire, and the understorey full of dead shrubs with harsh, scratchy twigs which left charcoal marks all over one's clothes. The ground was covered by a tinder-dry litter, full of spiky dead leaves and partly burnt branches, with no signs of the soft leaf mould and rotting trunks which cover the floors of English woods. Even the ground in the hills looked like a huge abandoned English gravel-pit, for those unfamiliar with laterite. However, my walks in Kings Park soon began to reveal the other side of the Australian bush: the beauty and harmony exhibited by an ecosystem which has evolved during an immense period of isolation from the rest of the world, making the best use of the local conditions.

Walking through Kings Park one of the first things I noticed was the extraordinary blackboys, or grass trees, which are one of the most characteristic plants of the Australian countryside. In late spring they project huge truncheon-like spikes of white flowers, which may be up to three metres tall. Surprisingly, they are related to the lily family, but evolved so long ago that they are regarded as a separate family now. The flowers are usually humming with insect activity, with many honeybees, solitary native bees, and some strange thynnid wasps, whose winged males are nearly always towing their tiny wingless females behind them as they feed on the flowers. Australian wall-butterflies (*Xenia*), and painted-lady butterflies are common, as well as hoards of ants.

With all this activity I wondered which insects were the main pollinators, but then it suddenly dawned that it was probably not an insect at all, as a large red wattle-bird came to feed from the flowers. Perhaps that is why the flowers are so tall and conspicuous — to attract honeyeaters, spinebills and wattle-birds from far and wide. They would then carry pollen on their feet and beaks over long distances, and ensure genetic diversity in the seeds. This method of pollination is unknown in Europe, where social bees are so abundant (although one bird-pollinated flower has recently been recognised — a kind of fritillary). Birds and mammals are very important pollinators in Australia, as there were no honeybees until they were brought in about 150 years ago. The kangaroo-paws are obviously adapted for bird pollination, because no nectar-seeking insect would go anywhere near the stamens. The flower-heads cleverly bend over to provide a suitable perch, while each flower bends out of the way after it has been pollinated to make way for the next flower.

The black trunks of blackboys show another interesting adaptation — to fire: the whole stem is clothed in a six-centimetre thick layer of leaf-bases glued together by a fire-retardant resin. The dead leaves stay attached to the plant as a skirt until they are burnt, so one can estimate when the last fire took place by the depth of skirt. If one cuts through the stem longitudinally it is found that the plants regularly produce flower buds, but they do not normally develop unless there is a fire; that is why one gets patches of blackboys all flowering at once. This strategy has presumably developed because the seedlings are only able to become established on recently burnt ground. It has been found that one can establish the fire history of an area by sectioning tall blackboys, which may be many hundreds of years old (they grow about 6 mm per year). This knowledge can be used to work out the best management regime to suit the native vegetation. All the vegetation was originally managed by the local Aboriginal population, and will only remain relatively unaltered if similar management can be actively reinstated. It is interesting that blackboys will sometimes flower in the city where they are not burnt — these plants tend to all flower at the same time, suggesting that certain unusual weather conditions can also trigger flowering activity.

In England I had always been fascinated by insectivorous plants — especially the sundews. In the Northern Hemisphere they grow in boggy areas where the water is so acid that dead plant material does not rot and instead accumulates into thick layers of peat. The nutrients become locked into the peat and are not available for plants to use for growth. The sundews are perfectly adapted to these places, because they obtain their minerals by catching nutrient-rich insects. I was astonished to find sundews growing everywhere in Kings Park — small ones with rosettes on the ground like the English ones, others with large ground-hugging leaves; then there were those with dense spikes of dew-covered leaves and the beautiful rambling kinds which festoon the vegetation with rainbows and showy flowers. This was not the habitat to expect to find sundews, yet they were everywhere. What I had not appreciated was that the Northern Hemisphere landscape was young and still had a blanket of rich glacial soils deposited over much of the area. Only a few places, like the acid bogs, had been in existence long enough for these insectivorous plants to colonise. In the Australian landscape, conditions were very different; the land surface is very ancient and made up of severely leached soils lacking mineral resources and trace elements. This is something which the early settlers did not appreciate either, to their cost. The native vegetation, on the other hand, shows a fascinating record of adaptation to these poor soil conditions. Sundews are just one of the many stories; they have flourished because they can outstrip other plants by getting ample nutrients from insects. About a hundred species are known in the world, half of which occur in Western Australia. Their advantage is lost, however, as soon as fertiliser is added to the soil; when this happens they are rapidly crowded out by exotic weeds and grasses. Like most bushland plants, they disappear from the vegetation after fertiliser application, almost as if a weedkiller had been applied.

I remember in the early '70s seeing my first pair of galahs at a nest in an old tuart branch. This bird is such a symbol of Australian wildlife that I was surprised not to see them everywhere in Perth, especially when I found that they were abundant in Adelaide and so could fully adapt to living in cities. What I had not appreciated was that I was in the middle of a very exciting biological event which is still occurring with great rapidity. The continent was only colonised 200 years ago, so the severe landscape changes associated with farming, forestry and pastoral industries only began to strike the West about the turn of the century and are still occurring. The galah was a bird adapted to arid central Australia, and has boomed into a pest because Western agriculture turns bushland and forest into a habitat very similar to its optimal desert conditions. The birds nesting in Kings Park were the vanguard of the population explosion which has now spread to most suburbs. South Australia in the early days elevated land clearance into an art form, and created its own little desert, and so it is not surprising that galahs spread into its cities before they did in Perth.

Other changes are occurring all the time in the animal and plant populations in the city. Ravens have only recently spread through the agricultural area and into the city, while the once common willy wagtails have all but disappeared due to the poisoning of their food supply by organochlorine insecticides used in the argentine-ant control program. These birds were beginning to return to some parkland areas, but further wholesale insecticide application is likely to prevent them from re-establishing. I was reminded of the time in 1960 when I walked on carpets of poisoned birds in England resulting from organochlorine pesticide use. It is interesting how materials known to be damaging continue to be used until they impinge on the seats of power. The dead birds did not seem to matter, but action was quickly taken when I found that foxes were dying from eating the dead birds. This was because many members of the House of Lords were fox-hunting people. Action on these chemicals did not occur in Australia until nearly twenty years later, when countries began to ban imports of our contaminated meat. The continued use of pesticides in the city probably helps to entrench a few hardy birds, like the crows and doves, and make the suburbs more open to invasion by exotic, city-adapted species such as sparrows and starlings.

After a while I began to look on Kings Park as a model which could be used to predict what may happen in natural bushland, because it has had the longest association with European culture without the more devastating effects of total land clearance or concreting over. Early descriptions show that the park was covered in tall timber and used by Aborigines to hunt kangaroos and wallabies with fire and spears. There were many animals and birds in the area not present now, such as bandicoots, native cats, whipbirds, bristlebirds and firetail finches. Even mallee fowl were thought to be present, although Gould could not find any in 1842. The last wallaby in the region was shot in 1905 in Mosman Park, and the last bilby (a bandicoot) was seen in 1928.

The trees disappeared at an early date through logging; old sawpits are dotted over the park, and the kangaroos were probably shot out at an early stage. At present the most obvious signs of change can be seen in the ground vegetation, because each year, and after each wildfire, the introduced species seem to become more firmly established. Gladioli have become so well entrenched that they appear on brochures as if they were native, instead of an invader from South Africa. Out of the 435 plants found in the park, mentioned in Eleanor Bennett's *The Bushland Plants of Kings Park,* 138 originate from outside Australia and another 13 are naturalised from other parts of the continent, like the kurrajong tree from New South Wales. The invading species include many grasses and plants belonging to the iris family, such as freesias and watsonias. Forty-three of the exotic species come from South Africa, which include some of the most invasive plants, probably reflecting the similar climatic conditions found in the Cape.

The most serious invader is veldt grass, which is ideally adapted to regular fires and flourishes at the expense of local species which need longer intervals between fires. I also suspect it of indulging in another form of warfare common in the plant world: of releasing toxic chemicals into the soil which kill competing plants. This would account for it tending to grow in almost pure stands in many suburban bush blocks. If left alone there is little doubt that it would replace almost the entire natural vegetation of the park — even the trees would eventually disappear with the lack of regeneration. Fortunately, the park authorities have an effective control program which is removing the plant from the bushland areas. It is hard to know what to do with the gladioli, watsonias and freesias. Many are rare in their native South Africa and, being escaped garden plants, they are attractive to the public; nevertheless, they are progressively squeezing the native flora out of the park. They do so well here because their natural enemies — burrowing and grazing mammals and a range of herbivorous insects — do not live here, while our native insects are not adapted to feeding on the exotic vegetation. One of their main enemies in South Africa is the golden mole, which feeds on the bulbs and corms, but if introduced here would probably cause a cane toad-like disaster.

Another worrying change is the state of the remaining tuart trees: they are so unhealthy that most have hollow branches which galahs can use as nest holes. Various theories have been advanced as to why they are declining. One suggestion has been that tree-felling and more frequent fires have opened up the canopy and allowed more dense ground vegetation to grow. This has the effect of increasing the rate of water loss, and of encouraging ground fires which singe the leaves of the remaining trees. Other suggestions point the finger at wood-boring beetles which are killing the branches, or at fungi which seem to be killing the trees, but these are more likely to be symptoms of malaise rather than the cause.

Work in New South Wales, where this problem is so widespread in gum trees that it is known as rural dieback, suggests there may be another reason, which is related to adaptation to poor soil conditions. It is a fascinating story of interrelated events. Because of the poverty of the Australian soils, gum leaves normally form a very poor diet for insects, which have a struggle to survive. However, when fertilisers are added by domestic stock, by air pollution (nitrates, sulphates and carbon dioxide) or as superphosphate, the leaves grow lush and become more nourishing for insects. As a result, the insects grow faster and fatter and lay more eggs. Normally, insect populations are controlled by predators such as birds and spiders, but when most of the land has been cleared the predator populations are less able to respond to insect abundance. Therefore, the insect populations erupt in these areas, defoliating the trees to such an extent that they sicken and die. We may be seeing something similar here in the tuarts. The insect populations may be booming because frequent fires are mobilising the soil nutrients and the area is being fertilised by increased carbon dioxide levels and sulphurous air pollution. At the same time many of the natural predators are declining because natural bushland plants are being replaced by exotic species, or because the effects of toxic sprays have largely removed birds like the willy wagtail.

It has been found that gum trees tend to have more insect-damaged leaves than trees do in Europe — it may be because the European trees have had time to adapt through a much longer association with Western agriculture and their adaptation to naturally fertile soils. However, European trees have their own problems of rural dieback now: elm-disease, oak-wilt, and now acid rain. Let's hope we can be spared from this last eventuality, but Kings Park suggests that although relatively few introduced species were able to invade Australia at first, a slower process of adaptation and attrition will lead to wholesale invasion in the long-term and to much of the Australian bushland being altered beyond recognition.

It is interesting to think that while the fertile glacial soils were being laid down in Europe, conditions were very different here. Kings Park would have been another forty kilometres further inland than it is now, and with the sea level being so much lower, the Swan River would have had quite a different look to it. Instead of the large flooded estuary we look down on now from Mt Eliza, the river would have been rushing through a deep gorge, discharging into the sea somewhere north-west of Rottnest Island. Glimpses of an even more distant past were found during the construction of The Narrows bridge when deep core samples were taken through layers of sediment to locate sites for the supporting piles. These cores cut through layers of peat which preserved the pollen grains of plant species living in the area millions of years ago.

The landscape was certainly very different 40 million years ago when, instead of the arid adapted vegetation seen now, the area supported lush swampy conditions with cool temperate deciduous rainforests of southern beech, *Livistona* palms and *Araucaria* pines. These forests extended over most of Western Australia, but were progressively restricted as the climate became more arid. The beech forests are now confined to Tasmania and parts of Victoria, with relic patches in the mountains of New South Wales and Queensland.

Some years ago I found some living evidence of this forest when sampling flying insects. The samples were being collected with the aim of monitoring changes occurring with increasing urbanisation and to document successive invasions by exotic species. Greenfly made up an important part of the catch and were nearly all imported species. However, there were some very interesting native species, including two new species identified for me by Dr Carver in Canberra. She was excited to find one which should have been living on southern beech, because all the others like it live on beech in Australia, New Zealand and South America. Presumably this one had managed to persist in Western Australia by switching from the declining beech trees to neighbouring swamp paperbarks.

Another trace was found at the foot of Kings Park, near the spring by the old brewery. A large spider was collected there in the 1860s, and when the museum specimen was later examined closely, it was found to have a tiny spider attached to its leg. The large trapdoor spider must have been walking amongst the ground vegetation and blundered through the small spider's web before it was caught. This small spider (*Chasmocephalon neglectus*) is the only specimen ever found of this species, but it has near relatives which only live in cool, damp, temperate rainforests. It must have been hanging on as a small population around the cool shady spring before the environment was irrevocably changed to a more arid climate through European management. The only similar place still remaining around the river is along the cliff face near Peppermint Grove where some of the pre-European vegetation persists, with *Callitris* pines and a shady spring with maidenhair ferns. This is all that is left of the scene found by Vlamingh when he first looked over the Swan River in December 1696, and came down to the spring near the yacht club, which was then thick with wildlife and birds — and signs of a rapid exodus by Aborigines, who must have viewed him like a visitor from outer space!

It is interesting to observe the changes which have been set in motion by European settlement and modern land usage. The changes seem slow to any individual, for instance, the changes in Kings Park in the twenty years since I first saw the place. These are mainly changes in abundance of native and introduced plants, with the addition of a few new species.

But the gross changes over a longer period are enormous, more like the vast changes in the past, such as from beech forest to seasonally arid jarrah/banksia woodland. Deep drilling for oil through the sediments below Perth provides us with details of other huge changes which have occurred in the past. After going through the beech forest era the drill soon strikes chalk. (One can see this formation near Gingin, where beautiful clear chalk streams run out of downland reminiscent of southern England. There are even areas of greensand like those of my familiar Surrey heaths.) The chalk was deposited by millions of microscopic organisms in the Cretaceous; it was a time of high sea levels and staggering diversity in animal life. Fossils found include some large marine dinosaurs and huge ammonite shells, which were squid-like animals. They lived in the oceans for about 300 million years but, like the dinosaurs and many of the microscopic organisms which formed the chalk, became extinct at the end of the chalk-forming era 66 million years ago. In geological terms this happened very abruptly all over the world, but "abrupt" in geological terms may be as much as a million years because time measurements are usually insufficiently accurate to register shorter time spans. Some geologists think the change may have only taken 10,000 years and was probably caused by a comet hitting the earth and creating either a nuclear winter or greenhouse effect, either of which could alter the world climate and ecology sufficiently to cause the mass extinctions. It is interesting that evidence suggests that the global climate was much warmer in the early Cretaceous, with an atmosphere containing more carbon dioxide than at present, creating a stronger greenhouse effect. Much of this carbon dioxide may now be locked away in the chalks and limestones deposited at the time.

Going deeper, the drill bit passes into Jurassic rocks, which can be seen at the surface in the Geraldton/Hill River area. These range in age from 208 to 144 million years and include fossil woods and coal measures. Below this, the drill passes through Triassic rocks 245–208 million years old and into Permian beds ranging from 286 to 245 million years old. This was an interesting time, when ice ages struck the world and deep swamps filled with peat, like those in the Canadian tundra at present. The weight of later rock formations crushed the peat into coal measures. Considerable quantities are present under Perth, but they are too deep down to be mined economically. The same formations are found in an isolated patch at Collie, where they are near enough to the surface for open-cut mining operations. The Permian ended with a mass extinction even more drastic than the one that ended the Dinosaurs.

At the bottom of the Permian the drill strikes hard igneous rocks similar to the ones which make up the Darling Scarp. These rocks were formed nearly 1,000 million years before the Permian sediments were deposited, but were probably above water for most of the time. They only plunged under the sea when the huge Darling Fault system developed, when cracks appeared in the Earth's surface and the rocks began to sink. They continued

Regrowth after fire in Kings Park. The first photograph was taken in March a few weeks after the fire when the casuarinas were just beginning to sprout. The second was taken in September during the spring and shows how rapidly the vegetation recovers after a fire, especially some of the South African weeds including freesias and gladioli.

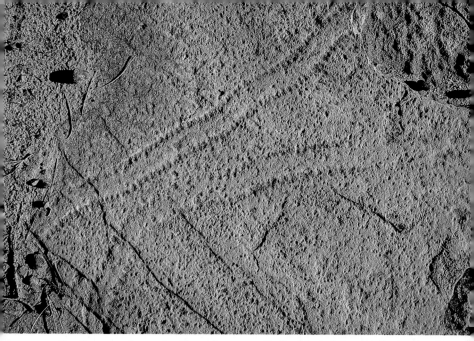

Fossil sea scorpion tracks. The rock strata under Perth include layers going back to the Permian period with many fossils. The rock strata come to the surface north of Perth such as the Cretaceous rocks at Gingin which have fossil ammonites and plesiosaurs. At Kalbarri even earlier rocks can be seen, such as this Devonian sandstone, walked over by long extinct sea scorpions.

Patersons's curse. Coming from the Mediterranean region this plan is well adapted to the Australian climate, and lacks its natural enemies. Plant invasions like this are not such a problem in Europe, possibly because the invasions took place long ago, especially during the Neolithic and Bronze Ages. These plants are now regarded as part of the natural flora, but some such as poppies are still a problem if herbicides are not used.

to sink with active movements in the faults until the Cretaceous. Less movement has occurred since then, but in all the base rock sank about seven kilometres from the surface.

The study of geology has always fascinated me, because the history of the earth is written in rock formations. However, it is a very frustrating record, because it is so difficult to read. When I studied the subject one of the key elements was missing — how to read the absolute age of rocks. It was quite clear that they were much older than implied in Genesis, but time spans in the fossil record were still guesswork, while little could be done with rocks covering most of the history of the planet, because they did not contain visible fossils. The Pre-Cambrian, 4,500–570 million years ago, was still a vast unknown territory.

Dating can now be done reasonably accurately, and it has become possible to compare what is happening now with changes which have occurred in the past. Timescales become all-important: the change from beech forest to savannah woodland took millions of years to occur, while it took about 100,000 years for the large mammals to die out, and 6,000 years for the Swan River gorge to flood. This can be compared with today, when even in our short lifetimes we can notice changes in the environment. This timescale provides a perspective to predict future consequences of the incredibly rapid change which is occurring now throughout the world. The change in the last 200 years in Australia is unprecedented and provides a fascinating insight into the ecological turmoil, which must be much worse than that which occurred at the end of the Permian and Cretaceous eras.

Driving east from Kings Park I crossed over the Causeway and was reminded of Levillain and Heirisson, who explored this area in 1801, and Captain Stirling, who in 1827 went with Frazer past Heirisson Island as far as Ellen Brook. They remark on the huge number of birds in the estuary, especially pelicans and black swans; Frazer records seeing 500 black swans at once. The River was very different then, being more protected from the sea, because there was a bar at Fremantle which cut out most of the tidal effects and prevented salt water from running back in summer to fill the deeper parts of the river. Daisy Bates even records that Aborigines caught gilgies (crayfish) at Heirisson Island. Fish were much more abundant, with the local Aborigines driving them in the same way as pelicans do, or using *gidgees* (spears) and small boomerang-like *kileys* to kill them. People recorded events such as a "plague" of snapper in Fremantle Harbour and a twenty-pound one caught off the Point Walter spit. The bar was removed in the 1890s and the river became more tidal and salty, with an airless layer forming in deep water. This layer has caused tides of dead fish from time to time, especially in 1955. Heavy fishing has also altered the river so much that some uneconomic species erupt in huge populations, such as "gobbleguts", which at one time became the main fish caught; later it was replaced by blowfish. The sea is no longer the only source of the salt in the estuary; the tributaries of the Avon have become more salty than the sea during summer through the effects of land clearance, although there was a similar time only 4,500 years ago caused by a period of drought when the Swan at Guildford was inhabited by marine shells.

Progressing along the Eastern Highway it is some time before one can see any vegetation again. The road gently undulates through the unplanned discord of used-car yards, fast-food outlets and advertising hoardings reminiscent of the worst of American small-town landscape architecture. The recent history of the area can still be glimpsed: a small patch of swamp with introduced reeds, canna lilies and watercress in the process of being filled in for an industrial complex, and a corner of a paddock full of capeweed and Paterson's curse with development "on hold" in case it is needed for a new freeway.

Some native she-oaks growing on the edge of the Swan River caught my eye, reminding me of more history to be found under the concrete. Records of the original vegetation still remain in the form of blackboy roots and banksia cones in the deep Bassendean sands, while the sand itself records an even more distant history; of a series of ice ages and intervening warm spells, like the one we have been experiencing over the last 10,000 years. During warm spells the sea level rises and at times has inundated the coastal plain and lapped at the base of the Darling Scarp. Sea shells and other marine organisms deposit lime on the sea bottom, which becomes exposed as the sea level drops at the onset of an ice age. Wind blows the exposed sand into extensive dune systems, which are consolidated into limestone by the action of rainwater; some of this limestone can be seen along Mounts Bay Road bordering Kings Park.

Having been deposited during a previous glaciation, the Bassendean sands are much older than the limestone in Kings Park. This has given the rainwater time to dissolve the calcium away, leaving behind a pure leached silica sand. Captain Stirling missed seeing this sand when he explored the fertile alluvial soils in the Swan Valley. If he had walked a little further and seen this infertile sand, he may not have been so enthusiastic about setting up the new colony, and avoided the great privations experienced during the early years.

Further east I found that the land was in the various stages prior to subdivision and concreting, with a few vineyards still in existence. Each year I notice that more vineyards disappear as land prices rocket and the vine leaves brown from the growing air pollution. The vintners must cast ever more envious eyes on their competitors who have moved far from the growing city to places such as Gingin, Mt Barker and Margaret River. In this relentless progression towards an urban fate, the end of the rural phase seems to be indicated when the land is let for horse grazing; this usually indicates that city investors and developers have acquired the land.

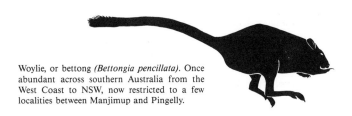

Woylie, or bettong *(Bettongia pencillata)*. Once abundant across southern Australia from the West Coast to NSW, now restricted to a few localities between Manjimup and Pingelly.

2 The Jarrah Forest Under Siege

The route into the hills took me along the Toodyay road past paddocks full of horses and blue with Paterson's curse from North Africa. Spring is a wonderful time of year, with colours surpassing anything found in Britain, but it is hard for me to come to terms with the fact that spring comes at the end of the growing season, and is not the start of life, bursting out after a long, cold, dreary English winter. The sky is so clear here and the sun so bright that the flowers almost fluoresce in the paddocks — brilliant yellow soursob, ochre-yellow capeweed, white, orange and pink watsonias, orange-red Cape tulips, white *Hesperantha falcata*, and patches of mauve and violet baboon flowers (*Babiana stricta*) as one drives up the escarpment. We have to thank South Africa for providing such an array of weeds to colour our cleared land, although I am not sure that the South Africans feel the same way about the Australian weeds which are spreading all over Cape Province. It is interesting that soursob does so well here in Australia, because it cannot spread by means of seeds. Many flowers have special adaptations to prevent them from pollinating themselves and soursob employs the same method as the primrose, using three different flower types. Pollination can only occur between plants with different flower types, but until recently only one flower type was present in Western Australia, so it mainly reproduces by means of bulbs.

Driving up the steep incline, I stopped at the top and walked to some weathered Devil's Marbles-like rocks overlooking the plain. The Darling Scarp is about 350 metres above sea level, and one can look right over the city to as far as Rottnest Island. This is the sort of place to which the human race seems to be drawn by some sort of innate behaviour — a form of habitat recognition going back to our origins on the open plains of Africa. We seem to love open spaces and arid landscapes with rock shelters overlooking plains. I suspect there is a strong link between the devastation of natural landscapes by Western culture and this inherited habitat-recognition originating in our distant ancestry. The world would be quite a different place if the gibbons had become the intelligent race: with their arboreal origins they would find beauty in trees and base their cultivation on forestry wherever they could grow trees. Conservationists would have to fight to preserve the arid open plains from ever-encroaching forests.

Increasingly, the view from the Scarp is obscured by what in England is known as haze, in Los Angeles as smog or generally as air pollution. It usually comes from fires: burning the bush is a national pastime, clearing the land for agriculture or for reducing the summer-fire hazard. But the growth of Perth is rapidly bringing about conditions which are likely to lead to smogs, because the weather patterns are very similar to those found in Los Angeles. The smoke condition has probably not changed much in the last few thousand years, as the Aborigines burned huge areas throughout the country every year. Vlamingh noted a great number of fires on the mainland on 29 December 1696, and early settlers recorded that annual burning usually started soon after Christmas.

It is salutary to think of these modern changes compared to the long history of the area. One can try to imagine looking down 100,000 years ago to the sea raging against cliffs at the base of the scarp, with salt spray drifting overhead, or 40 million years ago when one's view would be obscured by dense beech forest. More extraordinary things have happened in the more distant past: the presence of beech forests tells us that the climate was very different — rather like the climate found in England now, because Australia was much closer to the South Pole at that time. The fact that the whole continent has moved so far makes one realise how small we are and how puny are the forces we can muster. A hydrogen bomb only releases the energy of a very insignificant earthquake.

Some 280 million years ago there were probably some very severe earthquakes as the Darling Fault appeared and started moving. This is when the land west of Rottnest began sinking to form a rift valley like those in Africa. As time went on in the Permian, more land slips occurred like those one sees on the edge of a sandcastle hit by the rising tide, biting up to the base of the present Scarp. As soon as the first sections fell below sea level, at the start of the Permian, material carried from the scarp into the sea by rivers began to be deposited on it. It went on sinking, and built up the deposits mentioned in the last chapter. What is even more fascinating is what was beyond Rottnest, because there are no deposits before the Permian, so the land must have been above sea level then. Australia was then part of a huge land mass known as Gondwanaland which was made up of India, Africa, South America, Madagascar, New Guinea, New Zealand and Antarctica. Rift valleys appeared between the countries and filled with sea water, stretching out to become oceans. My view from the Scarp would have looked across the floor of a rift valley not to Rottnest, but to parts of the Indian subcontinent, possibly Tibet.

My gaze from a distant view of India, somewhere beyond Rottnest, was brought closer to hand by a noisy rustling sound in the shrubs; the sound of carefree breaking-wind instantly told me that it was a bob-tailed skink. One of the penalties of a vegetarian diet, used by elephant hunters to hear their quarry, is that it generates copious amounts of gases such as methane and carbon dioxide. This does not bother bobtails because they have no fear of predators. They have a very effective method of sham defence, even foxes seem to be put off by a huge lunging pink mouth and long blue tongue. However, this was no problem to the Aborigines who regularly preyed on them, so bobtails are probably one of the few animals which have benefited from European colonisation. This lizard is often called a "goanna" by Perth people, but the name is more generally used only for the Australian varanid monitor lizards. The origin of the word is presumably "iguana", which comes from the Carib name for a group of large lizards not found in Australia at all.

The bobtail stopped and began to eat some bright red flowers from a creeper on the ground. It was a scarlet-runner, one of a large variety of plants belonging to the pea family which grow in the jarrah forest. Round about I could see other pea flowers and it was interesting to note the array of colours; one wonders what insects they attract, or are they attracting birds? Red is one of the most frequent colours, often with a touch of orange and yellow. Bees' eyes do not see colours at the red end of the spectrum, so are unlikely to visit the flowers, while birds are very sensitive to red and visit a wide variety of red flowers, such as many bottlebrushes and Sturt's desert pea.

Another range of peas are mixtures of yellows and browns, including the "bacon-and-eggs" flowers. Many of these plants are highly toxic, the roots extracting fluorine from the laterite clays and storing it in their tissues as fluoracetic acid. The other main colour adopted by peas seems to be mauve or purple, often in early flowering varieties such as the hoveas. This reminded me of flowers in England, which tend to be white and yellow early in the year, moving to mauves in late spring. It is fascinating when looking at flowers closely to think that each one is cleverly and precisely designed to achieve pollination, because the process of natural selection has ensured that only those which attract pollinators produce seeds. Many are attractive to our eyes, but others have colours in the infra-red and ultraviolet parts of the spectrum invisible to our eyes, or have been diverted along lines which are equally effective for pollination yet do not involve bright colours at all.

The bobtail passed by a greenish yellow plant sticking out of a damp piece of turf overlying a rocky slope. Looking closely, I saw that it was an elbow orchid in full flower. This is one of an array of strange orchids unique to Western Australia, which dupe male wasps into pollinating the flowers. Part of the flower mimics the wingless female wasp, and even emits the right sex attractant scent. The males fly up to the flower and grab hold of the "female" and try to fly off with it. But the flower is hinged so that the wasp swings upward and is neatly clasped with its back against the pollen and stigma. It rests a while trying to attend to its "female", then flies off — with pollen attached — to find the next "mate". These flowers have another extraordinary adaptation: growing in places which rapidly dry out at the time of year when the wasps fly, they need to avoid desiccation. They do this by storing enough water in the stem, and do most of the growing and flowering after the base of the stem has died. This disconcerted early botanists who tried to press the flowers, only to find that they continued to grow in the flower-press.

Looking around I could see other orchids: the beautiful tall blue-lady orchid, yellow cowslip orchids, donkey orchids amongst the rocks, and a dull green species from South Africa which has become fully established here. Round about there were many other plants in flower; several kinds of trigger plants, yellow hibbertias, orange sundews, feather flowers, melaleucas, dryandras, petrophiles and a host of other kinds. The South-west has a remarkably rich flora, with over 4,000 native species. This slope next to the jarrah forest made the downland flora of southern England with its orchids, thyme, marjoram and gentians seem very poor in comparison. In a little remnant of forest near Gidgegannup I have found twenty-nine kinds of orchid alone, and each year I add a few more: there could easily be another twenty growing in the area.

Various explanations have been offered for such a great variety of plants found in Western Australia, but it appears that it has a lot to do with periods of drought during ice ages. Drought creates a very disjointed environment, with small patches of suitable soil conditions well separated from one another by inhospitable drought-prone country. This means that plants which could be widespread during the warm–wet interglacial periods become isolated in many island-like populations. If the drought lasts long enough, these populations evolve into separate species, which remain intact when the wetter conditions return. But there are also other reasons which are mentioned in later chapters.

The soil in the jarrah forest forms a very distinct habitat compared to neighbouring areas. The granite rocks have been subject to deep weathering, with the surface being protected by a hard layer of laterite cap rock. The laterite is added to each time there are long dry periods which evaporate the water held in the deep soils below and the dissolved (colloidal) solids are deposited at the surface. The solids brought to the surface are mainly iron and aluminium compounds, while white sands and china clay are left in the lower levels. Where the aluminium content is high, the material is known as bauxite and is open to mining operations.

It was interesting that during the exploration phase prospectors found that jarrah could be used as an indicator for bauxite deposits. This tree has a wide range, extending from east of Esperance up to Eneabba, and may have a growth form ranging from a small mallee to a giant forest tree. But it was discovered that in the forest area where bauxite is found, those places which had the best jarrah trees were those with the deepest bauxite deposits. Cutting through the soil to reveal the roots shows why; it is because they have a unique rooting system. The bauxite soils may be as deep as 30 metres and hold a huge reserve of water at the base in sands and china clay. The jarrah trees have no need to adapt to the long summer droughts, because they have special roots which sink down vertically and tap this water resource. This enables them to grow and flower during the summer months, even though there may be no rain between December and April.

Thinking of the jarrah reminded me of a time when I walked through an area of the Lane Poole National Park near Dwellingup. I had been asked for some photographs of jarrah trees, but when I started looking, I found it very hard to find good examples, even though it was in the centre of the forested area. Mostly the trees were small, staggy and deformed, or obscured by heavy regrowth. I kept on coming across huge stumps, which gave an idea of what had been there before the loggers came. In the end I did find some of these veritable giants still standing, which had probably been saved by having a hollow or twisted trunk. It is salutary to think that in only 150 years of European colonisation, half the forest has been cleared for agriculture and virtually all the rest has been logged. As a result the forest is a very different place from when the first Europeans came. Then there was a tall dense canopy made up of well-spaced giant trees, which probably cut light penetration sufficiently to prevent a dense understorey growing, except where an old giant died leaving a temporary clearing. People describe how one could walk or ride through the forest as if it were a deer park. The logging operations have removed the high canopy and opened the forest as if it were a large clearing, bringing about a dense growth of ground vegetation and young trees. This encourages fires, which can flare up high enough to damage the short young trees even during cool spring burns, and result in the staggy-looking forest.

I would like to think that we are in an age of rational science-based technology, but I am continually reminded that what we do is firmly based in long-established traditions. Our science seems to be largely used to make our traditional practices more efficient; it rarely achieves radical changes. This is well illustrated by forestry. The role of government in forestry goes back to the Dark Ages, when kings needed to secure a source of venison and timber to pay debts, particularly when they were short of money. They drew lines on a map and decreed the area a Royal Forest; that is, a place where Forest Law applied. It did not mean that the area was covered in trees — they were mainly open heathland areas, like the New Forest created in 1087 by William the Conqueror. In fact, Robin Hood probably had some difficulty finding trees in Sherwood Forest in which to hide from the Sheriff. Since then there has been an evolution in the understanding of forestry, from a place where kings could get commodities (mainly deer) to a place where timber grows for the benefit of governments. We still seem to assume unconsciously that forestry is something special, practised by kings to create wealth. This assumption has been at the root of the demise of huge areas of some of the most valuable landscape features of the British countryside this century, when the government saw a strategic need for timber. Heaths, commons, moors, woods, and bogs which had developed a rich vegetation over thousands of years of local human management, were bulldozed or drained and planted with exotic conifers by the Forestry Commission. The cost was so enormous that the government finally had to listen to the economists. In some areas deer exclusion costs were shown to exceed the value of the timber being protected and the forests are now used for producing venison as in the old days.

Our forest management appears to have been pervaded by a similar outlook, with frequent evidence of tree-farming operations in the form of coniferous plantations scattered through the jarrah forest, and signs of costly government management. Hopefully, this can change without further forest destruction, because no money can buy back jarrah forest once it has been cleared. Future generations are going to set a great premium on natural areas, and the creation of the Lane Poole National Park within the forest is a hopeful sign that at least some of this invaluable resource may be managed more for the next century, instead of only for the woodchip and timber requirements of the present.

Another feature of the British scene is very relevant to understanding the jarrah forest. From about 6,000 years ago Stone-Age man began clearing British primeval forests (wildwood), and it was virtually complete long before the Romans arrived. We tend to think of oak and beech as being the forest trees of England, but the now rare small-leaved lime (known as "Pry") was the dominant tree, with elm, ash and hazel. Oak and beech did better on poorer soils but, with managed grazing in woodland, were able to spread at the expense of the other trees. Elm was lost as a woodland tree, hazel became shrub-like and the "Pry" disappeared altogether. Before this time there had of course been an ice age, when the country was largely tundra, as well as many thousand years of Mesolithic human occupation, when many of the important grazing animals were driven to extinction.

The jarrah forest has not experienced a Neolithic-like land clearance for farming and grazing domestic stock, but it has had at least 40,000 years of profound human influence, especially through hunter-gathering, fire management and its associated grazing effects, and through the extinction of some of the larger grazing mammals. It has also been through a period of serious drought, when the sea receded during the last ice age and the climate became more drought-prone. This means that the forest is now in a state of flux, perhaps like the one the British countryside has gone through recently. The Industrial Revolution, two World Wars and myxomatosis released the countryside from traditional land management, which lasted with little change for thousands of years. This resulted in an incredible blooming of the woods, heaths and downlands forty years ago. Unfettered growth since then has meant that the British woods have now lost their aconites and primroses, while the heaths and downland are fast becoming woods. Perhaps we are seeing something similar in the jarrah forest now. The mass flowering of the ground vegetation may be a result of the release from Aboriginal management, or may be from changes after timber mining

Thorny bitter pea. One of the many kinds of pea family plants growing in the jarrah forest which have orange-brown flowers; some contain toxic fluoroacetic acid. Presumably some insect pollinator is particularly attracted to this colour, and is not affected by the poison.

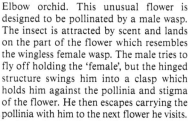

Elbow orchid. This unusual flower is designed to be pollinated by a male wasp. The insect is attracted by scent and lands on the part of the flower which resembles the wingless female wasp. The male tries to fly off holding the 'female', but the hinged structure swings him into a clasp which holds him against the pollinia and stigma of the flower. He then escapes carrying the pollinia with him to the next flower he visits.

Scented orchid. Many kinds of ground orchid are found in the jarrah forest, some using exotic ways of achieving pollination, like the elbow orchid, others using bees like the blue lady orchid. The scented orchid is unusual because it pollinates itself; in fact some variants do not open their flowers at all.

Yellow banjine. One of the huge variety of flowers found on the floor of the jarrah forest which includes pink and white banjines. They have a very tough bark, especially the large benjine found in the karri forest which was used to make rope in the early days.

Huge jarrah tree. The first settlers would have found the jarrah forest quite different from that seen now. Nearly all the forest has been logged, so the large trees like this have gone. In their place is a relatively thick regrowth of younger trees, or sprouting stumps. Sometimes one can find fire-scarred tree remnants which may be over a thousand years old. Repeated fires have burned out the original trunks, but the bases continue to grow and produce a ring of trees many metres in diameter.

Jarrah dieback. Apart from the invasion by exotic plants and disturbance caused by logging, the forest is under severe pressure from an exotic fungal disease which kills about 60 per cent of the flora. Banksias are particularly susceptible, jarrah less so. Trees usually die during the summer when the disease cuts off the water supply to the tree, and the dying trees are easy to recognise by their brown leaves.

Pygmy possum. The jarrah forest used to have a rich mammal fauna, but many of the native species are now rare. This possum is still found in parts of the forest, especially near creeks with plenty of banksia trees. Jarrah dieback is likely to remove much of its remaining habitat.

operations over the last hundred years. Perhaps some other trees may have been dominant had there been no human interference? We await studies on pollen found in peat deposits to tell us more about vegetation changes in the past.

Some jarrah trees are incredibly old, despite frequent fires; walking through the forest one often comes across trees which have repeatedly regrown from an original rootstock that may be as much as seven metres across and many thousands of years old, like the "coppice stools" in England. An interesting change due to the loss of Aboriginal management has been found in the little tree *Persoonia elliptica*. Hardly any have regenerated since before the turn of the century because grazing pressure by kangaroos increased when they were no longer hunted by Aborigines, and most new trees were eaten.

One of the things which has made fire so important in the jarrah forest is that the laterite soil is very poor. It is particularly deficient in nitrogen, and the phosphorus it contains is very hard to extract. The nitrogen mainly comes from the wealth of pea plants and wattles which can fix nitrogen from the air using nitrogen-fixing bacteria. Other plants can do this as well, such as the macrozamia palm and she-oaks. In damp climates fungi rot vegetation so that minerals can be returned to the soil, but rotting barely occurs here, so plants have to rely on periodic fires to incinerate the vegetation and return nutrients to the soil. Hence there are complex adaptations to fire such as oils deposited in discarded gum leaves to encourage fire, fire resistant bark and seeds which are only dropped after fires or have food packages on them to encourage ants to store them underground out of the reach of flames. There is also a system of roots to rapidly collect released nutrients, often aided by close association with soil fungi.

Most plants have what are known as mycorrhizal associations with fungi. It is a sort of symbiosis where the fungi have a close relationship with plant roots and pass nitrogen and phosphorus on to the plants. The exchange is complex, almost making it appear as if the forest is a closely interlocking community, because radioactive isotopes placed in one tree very quickly appear in its neighbours, passed on via the mycorrhizal fungi. This system can easily be disrupted: timber extraction bodily removes nutrients and, as in tropical rainforests, it is unlikely that jarrah forest can sustain removal indefinitely, as the English woods can, growing on their rich glacial soils. It can also be disrupted by changing the fire regime. The forest burns best during the summer drought, when there probably would have been natural lightning strikes. The Aborigines also burnt it at that time of year (fire was presumably more controllable then, because there was less ground vegetation and a high canopy). These fires are hot and most plants have seeds which only germinate after hot fires, especially the nitrogen-fixing acacias and legumes. "Prescribed burning" in the forest changed the season of burning mainly to cool spring fires, which instead of encouraging the soil-fertilising legumes, favoured marri trees and bull banksia which now form thick stands in many places.

This burning program has been partly responsible for jarrah trees dying in upland areas, through a complex network of factors. Many exotic species have found their way to Western Australia, and one is probably the most disastrous pathogen known to affect natural ecosystems. It is known here as jarrah dieback disease and is caused by a fungus first found in cinnamon in Indonesia (*Phytophthora cinnamomi*). It is also affecting Victorian forests and is widespread in nurseries and orchards. It has entered the web of roots and fungi in the soil and kills 60 per cent of the forest flora, especially plants in the Proteaceae such as bull banksia. Jarrah is relatively resistant to the disease but cannot cope in the wetter soils found in valleys and slopes, where the fungus invades all its surface roots. The fungus cannot survive in dry soils, so it should not affect jarrahs in upland areas. However, in very wet periods, pools of water collect on the top of the laterite cap rock up to a metre below the surface. This is where the jarrah water-seeking roots penetrate holes and dive down to the water table. If cool burning has taken place, there may be many bull banksias in the area which can become heavily infected by the fungus. They then pass the disease on to jarrah at the point where it can least afford damage — its life sustaining water supply roots. Fire management is now changing to include hot fires where possible; not only do these discourage the disease-harbouring bull banksia, but they encourage soil enriching legumes and wattles such as prickly moses. It has also been found that prickly moses is doubly valuable, because it exudes a chemical into the soil which discourages jarrah dieback fungus.

With the forest one sees today one wonders what far-reaching effects there have been from timber extraction and cool spring burning. It is easy to see changes in the bird fauna after burns or logging, when robins come in and wrens move out, but what happens to the insects? One wonders whether the cool burns and logging have anything to do with the huge outbreak of jarrah leaf miners. The caterpillars of this moth burrow in jarrah leaves and have erupted to such an extent that trees are defoliated over large areas, contributing to the general malaise of the forest.

I am reminded that constant and often profound changes are still in the process of occurring in the jarrah forest. My patch of forest at Gidgegannup had perhaps as many as thirty brush wallabies on it twenty years ago; very

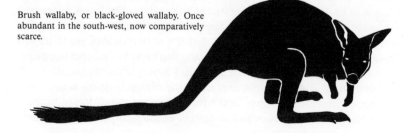

Brush wallaby, or black-gloved wallaby. Once abundant in the south-west, now comparatively scarce.

occasionally we saw a grey kangaroo and a couple of relic emus. Nearly all the surrounding forest has now been cleared, taking the emus with it and the wallabies have declined almost to extinction — there may be two left. Their place has been taken by about forty kangaroos. We read in textbooks how many mammals have declined or become extinct in the past, but most people do not realise that most of the decline took place quite recently, even in living memory. It is barely appreciated that the wallaby was the most abundant species in the forest only fifteen years ago, but may now be well on its way to extinction on the mainland. It used to be one of the most frequent animals killed on the roads, probably doing well while the forest shrub layer blossomed. Hardly anything is known about the animal, because it is very hard to capture and I do not know why it has declined. It may be due to changes in the ground vegetation; the unusually dense vegetation caused by spring burns and defoliation may have encouraged the species outside its normal range, and the population twenty years ago may have been unnaturally high, or it could be due to fox predation, as with the woylie, which is discussed below. Who knows?

One of the strange relics in the jarrah forest is the population of woylies in the Perup area east of Manjimup. This is a most unexpected place to find one of the last remaining populations of this little rat-kangaroo, because it was mainly a semi-desert species which ranged across the Nullarbor to South Australia. It was even considered a serious pest by early wheat growers. Something in the Perup allowed it to persist when it died out everywhere else; the food and habitat were probably not really to its liking, but it seems as if it survived because the ground vegetation made it difficult for foxes to catch it. This is one of the extraordinary things about nature which is obvious when one thinks about it; animals and plants can live in a very wide range of conditions well outside their normal range — zoos, botanical gardens, fields and forests, providing they are protected from things which eat them, or compete with them. But in the natural environment normal ecological forces come into play, and restrict distributions. Another good example is given by the quokka, which is discussed in Chapter 12. This is a small marsupial which lives in dense swamps on the mainland, and in a desert-like area on Rottnest Island where there are no predators or competitors present to restrict it.

One of the things which allowed the woylie to persist at the Perup seems to have been that there was a good supply of truffles and other ground fungi for it to feed on, particularly after fires. The forest there must still have a healthy mycorrhizal association, but one wonders whether it may have been lost further north where there are no woylies and few truffles.

Apart from forestry, one of the main uses to which the forest has been put is the provision of water, many valleys having been flooded with reservoirs. In the early days attempts were made to increase the water run-off into the reservoirs by clearing the forest around the area. However, this was soon stopped when it was found that the amount of salt in the run-off was greatly increased. Extensive replanting is now in progress, to try and improve water quality. It is often assumed that salt in the ground comes from the groundrock weathering, but in fact it mainly comes from rain. The ocean spray dries to produce minute salt crystals which produce a haze in the atmosphere and act as nuclei for the formation of water droplets in clouds. In high rainfall areas, salt in the rainwater runs into rivers and back out to sea, but where there is low rainfall, most is retained in the soil and builds up until the amount leaving equals the amount falling. This build-up of salt rises dramatically as one travels further east, and corresponds with lower rainfall, so that during the ice age drought, salt accumulation occurred much closer to the present coast. It is interesting that these factors led to the gold deposits at Boddington. During the ice age droughts, the goldfield area was desert-like, with severe dust storms ripping over it. Heavy-metal bearing dusts were deposited over the Darling Range — and even as far as Antarctica, where higher levels of lead have been found in ice from this period. Gold, being soluble in salt, was transported from this dust and the weathered rock by the saline water and deposited into the layer which is now mined.

The jarrah forest has a great variety of soil types, and one keeps stumbling upon little patches with unique vegetation, such as a clay swamp full of showy bladderworts or a rocky outcrop with ferns and feather flowers, and open areas with a white sandy soil. The sand patches are rather interesting because they may be a link with the coal measures at Collie. They could be glacial in origin, being the remains of Permian ice age deposits dating from the time when Australia was still connected to Antarctica. It is strange that near Boddington there is a population of a rare scorpion-fly. This particular species belongs to one of the most ancient groups of insects known, found as fossils from the early Permian, and is only known

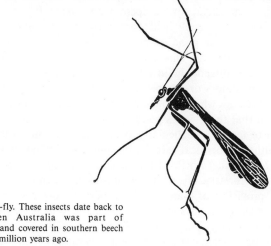

Harpy Scorpion-fly. These insects date back to the time when Australia was part of Gondwanaland and covered in southern beech forests, over 40 million years ago.

from a few living specimens in Western Australia and another related species in the eastern part of America. This was a time when insects were evolving into the modern families and were active in the glossopteris flora preserved in the coal at Collie.

Standing up and walking away from the devil's marbles I disturbed another insect. It was the more modern harpy scorpion-fly, which dates back only 40 million years to the southern beech forests which preceded the jarrah forest. I wondered if it will survive as a species to see the next forest, evolving from the jumble of species we have brought here from all over the world.

White-tailed black cockatoos. Two species are recognised in Western Australia: the long-billed form and the short-billed form. They do not interbreed, although hard to tell apart.

3 The Wheat-Belt: Total Land Clearance.

Driving on through our remaining "wildwood" of jarrah forest towards the wheat-belt, I saw the undergrowth become thinner and more grass-like, particularly where it grows on areas of white sand near Mt Dale on the Brookton Highway. Some of this thinning is due to jarrah dieback disease, which only leaves the grass-like monocotyledonous plants behind. Plantations of resistant eucalypts from other parts of Australia and pine trees show where foresters have tried to develop a timber crop in infected areas.

After about sixty kilometres of driving, the green semi-shade of the trees abruptly gives way to dazzling, straw-covered paddocks, which shimmer in the summer heat. Going back to the old records, one realises that it was a grassy appearance which attracted the settlers to this area in the first place. Despite the gulf between the Stone-Age Aboriginal people and the invading British culture, they shared the same recognition of habitat. An Aboriginal population was concentrated in this area, and the British colonisers immediately recognised the area as relatively good farming country, compared with the sterile Bassendean Sands and jarrah forest laterite. In fact the grassy, park-like appearance had been created by thousands of years of Aboriginal management. A similar effect was created by Red Indians along the eastern edge of the Great Plains, and one wonders how much of the African grasslands are the product of management by the indigenous peoples, who burn the grasslands, encouraging the game both to concentrate in the burnt areas and to graze on the regrowth, weeding out encroaching bushland. These grasslands soon become thorn-scrub in the absence of fire and grazing, like that developing on the slopes of the Drakensberg Mountains.

Aboriginal management of the area was not a haphazard process, but well planned and based on as much as a 40,000-year history of experience. The traditional management had evolved as the most effective means of living off the country, in the same way as our agricultural practice goes back through thousands of years of experience. The management was most obviously through burning; each Aboriginal group was responsible for its own territory because their lives depended upon it. They would have known each part of it in great detail, its fire history and when it was due for burning. Fires were set during the dry summer months, starting towards the end of December. Experience provided a control on the areas burned, particularly the weather conditions and the locations of previous burns. The burns were used to drive game, but in the process removed scrub and stimulated grasses which attracted kangaroos. Unfortunately, we do not know much about this fire management, so do not know the conditions which led to the present tree cover and vegetation of the area. Hopefully, future studies will find suitable swamp deposits, such as those at Lake George in New South Wales, which will show what vegetation changes have taken place and provide details of the frequency of fires.

Fire is the most obvious influence on the countryside, but all the other activities of these hunter-gatherers must also have had a strong influence on the land. It is hard to know what, but they certainly had a strong influence on some important species, such as macrozamia palms (a kind of cycad). Some of the burning was done with the express aim of making these plants produce cones so that the Aborigines could eat the seeds, but it also helped to increase the number of "palms". Other activities included the encouragement of yams (*Dioscorea*) in areas where they grew and the killing of grass trees to encourage "bardie grubs". There is little doubt now that the final extinction of the large herbivorous marsupials was largely brought about by human activities, partly by hunting and partly by changing the vegetation.

One therefore has to appreciate that the wildwood is a product of Aboriginal influence, not just in changing the structure and species composition of the vegetation but also at the more profound level of natural selection within species, because even the most long-lived forest trees have gone through at least 200 generations since Aborigines started using fire in the area. So every species would have had time to perfect its adaptations to this form of management, or become extinct.

The British settlers had a different view of the bushland; they saw it through the eyes of people familiar with deer parks in the English countryside, and perhaps felt they could achieve some of the wealth denied to them by the park-owning upper classes in England. Meanwhile the planners in Perth saw the rosy glow of a city growing through a hinterland of expanding agriculture, and quickly dissected the country with property boundaries like the ones they were familiar with back home This was the time of the Enclosure Acts in England, which saw the remaining open areas of Britain being fenced off to become private property. It was done from maps without regard for topographical details, or for the future need of public areas. This planned landscape remains today as the boring parts of the English countryside which one has to drive through on the way to the more scenic older landscapes. (However, even planned landscapes can become attractive in the long-term, like those parts of the English countryside which still retain the regimented fields planned thousands of years ago by unknown Neolithic masters.)

It is a pity that the local Aborigines were not allowed any input into the planning of the wheat-belt; if they had, we would now see a fascinating mosaic of modern farming within a framework of prehistory. As it is, the fencelines have no sympathy with the landscape, marching straight up hills and even through the centre of salt lakes, while the only bushland remaining survives because planners saw the need for such modern requirements as gravel reserves for road building and mallee reserves to provide pit-props for mining. Largely, it is an unforgiving desert for much of the year, increasingly plagued by problems resulting from the decades of over-exploitation forced on the area by modern agriculture. Some of the problems can be traced to the small size of what was considered to be a self-supporting unit in the original subdivisions, and to the conditions of the leases which required that the bushland should be completely cleared within a specified time. The last anachronism remained until very recently, even though it was hard fought against by those who foresaw today's problems; people were not even allowed to keep bushland so that they could farm it for its flowers. The problem with salination was well known in the 1950s, with soil scientists urging immediate action to curb unsympathetic land clearance, yet the million-acres-a-year clearance policy did not come to an end until the late 1970s.

When driving through the wheat-belt, it is hard to come to terms with the fact that the land clearance was largely a modern phenomenon, either completed within living memory or still occurring on the fringes. Only a relatively small area was cleared by the turn of the century and the isolated salmon and york gums at the roadside are the survivors from the original clearance. In the early days, salmon gums were so numerous that no-one thought to try to preserve them; they merely indicated where clearing should begin, because they grew on the best agricultural land. They were like the jarrah trees which indicate where the best bauxite is to be found. The Christmas tree was the only kind which had any protective legislation, due to its attractive flowers — not because it is a root parasite which attacks grasses in the paddocks! Now the last survivors of all the original trees are succumbing to salination, road-widening, ringbarking by hungry stock, and loss from phosphate poisoning or herbicide drift, while very little unaided regeneration takes place because of the continued grazing pressure from stock and rabbits.

Fortunately, human and monetary values change with the times. Now there is a concern over the future of wheat-belt farming and growing tourism which demands bushland flowers at least along roadsides. These new values have led a growing number of farmers and councils to invest money in protecting native trees and on planting new ones with government support.

Salmon gum *(Eucalyptus salmonophloeia)*. This was a tree characteristic of the better soils in the wheat-belt region, and for this reason most salmon gum woodlands have been cleared for agriculture. Only a few trees remain along roadsides and for shelter in paddocks. They will die out in time unless farmers actively plant new trees and protect them from grazing stock.

West Australian Christmas tree. This tree belongs to the mistletoe family, and because of its attractive flowers has been protected from clearance in agricultural areas. Many paddocks in the wheat-belt still contain patches of these trees, which persist by parasitising the roots of grasses.

Heath vegetation in the wheat-belt. Sandy heaths contain a wide variety of plants which produce a rich display of flowers during the spring. These feather flowers are particularly attractive in the Lake Grace area.

Mistletoe caterpillar *(Comocrus behri)*. If one looks closely at the ecology of any animal or plant one finds there is a complex interaction between apparently unrelated factors. Mistletoe is a parasite and can kill trees if too abundant; but it is eaten by many mistletoe-eating insects. Mistletoe birds carry seeds a long way, so some grow where there are no mistletoe insects. The trees depend on insects like this moth finding the parasite before they succumb. (Other mistletoe relationships are given in my book *Flower Power*).

Gungurru *(Eucalyptus caesia)*. This gum is commonly grown in gardens now, but originates on a few rocky outcrops in the wheat-belt, such as at Boyagin Rock near Brookton. With such a specific habitat the trees on each rocky outcrop are isolated from the others and have become genetically different. This is the way in which most new species are formed.

Lace lichen. This attractive lichen is characteristic of rocky outcrops in the wheat-belt. It grows during the winter months when it becomes soft and pliable, but dries out during the summer, becoming crisp underfoot.

Salt-affected land. Most lakes and swamps in the wheat-belt area have become saline since the land was cleared. The salt was already present in the soil, deposited in rain during the last several thousand years. This salt was in equilibrium until the land was cleared, when deep-rooted plants were removed and run-off increased. The salt collects in swamps, many of which used to have freshwater, and kills the trees.

Banjo frog. Most frogs have suffered as a result of land clearance in the wheat-belt, especially the spotted frog which can only breed in the sort of swamps which are prone to become salty. The banjo frog, on the other hand, bred in freshwater running off granite outcrops, and found that farm dams were ideal breeding sites. It is now very common and has spread to lakes around Perth.

However, it was hard for some people to escape the deeply ingrained association of tree-planting with money-making forestry and one regularly sees regimented pine plantations and shelterbelts.

In the early days of clearance, the farmers had to cope with a menagerie of wildlife, with such animals as rat-kangaroos (woylies and boodies) in such pest proportions that they lost their crops. As the land was cleared, whatever wildlife was in it had to move or die, and the remaining bushland probably became temporarily overcrowded, so that some animals had to rely on neighbouring crops for food until the population density returned to normal. It is distressing to think that when a farmer clears a 100-hectare paddock, he is instrumental in killing the entire bird fauna of perhaps 150 species with 1,000 individuals, let alone the entire ecosystem of millions of plants, insects, mammals, soil fauna and microbes.

The woylies and boodies have gone now, and many others of the once-abundant wheat-belt animals are now extinct or restricted to offshore islands. The process continues today, with many more species about to become extinct, at least locally. White-tailed black cockatoos were in recent years one of the features of the wheat-belt. These beautiful, intensely social birds fly in graceful flocks flowing over the countryside with constant liquid communications and seemingly playful aerobatics. They have nearly disappeared now, because most of the banksias and hakeas on which they feed have gone, while their nest holes are now taken by the desert-loving galah. One result of their loss is that many of the remaining banksias cannot produce seed, and are likely to die out because there are no longer any cockatoos to break open flowers and remove weevil larvae. These weevils are now so abundant that every seed head is eaten out, and none set seed. This may lead to a snowball effect on the honeyeaters which rely on banksias for food. Natural ecosystems are made up of a complex network of interdependent relationships such as these, so that even minor interference may have far-reaching and unexpected results.

Many remaining areas of bushland give the illusion that they are little changed since European settlement. This is because the individual plants became established when most of the ecosystem was still intact; bushland plants generally being so long-lived. The same applies to many of the remaining animals and birds, which are surprisingly long-lived, such as adult trap-door spiders, which persist in areas long after they have become so changed that no young spiders could survive. The process of fundamental change is sweeping through all areas of natural bushland. This change began with the loss of Aboriginal influence and most of the native mammals, and was compounded by the invasion by exotic species such as cats, foxes, rabbits and agricultural weeds. As time passes, ageing animals and plants will not be replaced and more and more links in the original network will be severed. It will take thousands of years for these changes to work through the system and for new links to be forged so that new complex ecosystems can be constructed. The chalk downland vegetation in southern England gives us

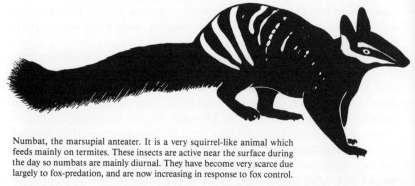

Numbat, the marsupial anteater. It is a very squirrel-like animal which feeds mainly on termites. These insects are active near the surface during the day so numbats are mainly diurnal. They have become very scarce due largely to fox-predation, and are now increasing in response to fox control.

an idea of what can appear in time; it is hard to appreciate that this beautiful ecosystem has such a devastating past. It is the result of Neolithic people hacking down the majestic wildwood about six thousand years ago and introducing a plethora of exotic agricultural weeds from the tundra and Middle East. It was then moulded by thousands of years of grazing by domestic animals to yield a beautiful turf with its own complex flora and fauna. Sadly, most of it has been lost in the last forty years through modern agriculture and forestry and from a dense thorn-scrub which grows as soon as chalk-grassland is released from grazing pressure. One wonders what the new ecosystems will look like in Western Australia, when they have had time to evolve?

Few large reserves remain in the wheat-belt, some of the best being at Boyagin, Tutanning and Dryandra. When I first saw these reserves, the numbat was still quite common and I even saw one crossing the road near Armadale. I was surprised how squirrel-like the animal was, even though it is a marsupial anteater. At Tutanning they regularly crossed the tracks in full view, brandishing squirrel-like tails as if inviting me to chase them. It seems as if they have been forced to become diurnal, even during the parched heat of summer, because termites are mainly active near the surface during the daytime. But, like squirrels, they appear to have little fear of predators because they are thoroughly familiar with their territory and at the first sign of danger can dash for the safety of a treehole or hollow log. This may have been their downfall, because foxes and cats are remarkably good at catching squirrels, and numbats had never been exposed to such efficient ground predators before.

Both woylies and numbats used to range right across Australia but declined dramatically, particularly after the 1930s. Initially it was thought that the rabbit was one of the main influences, particularly in the desert areas, where habitat was rapidly eaten out. But work on the rock wallaby suggests that the fox was the final straw. This wallaby used to be widely distributed on rocky outcrops through the wheat-belt but now only survives on a few. It was lost at Boyagin long ago. Some populations were studied by Jack Kinnear, who found that they were declining with no young being added to the population. He then tried removing fox-predation by poisoning and soon found that young rock wallabies were surviving, and the population began to boom again. This work was extended to the numbats at Dryandra, which increased to such an extent that excess animals were produced. These have been released at Boyagin, where a new population has now been established. The woylies at Dryandra and Tutanning clearly need similar protection to persist — at least until the population can adapt to the new predator and the altered ecosystem.

Most people recoil at the idea of using poison as a conservation measure. It seems to be a contradiction in terms. However, there is a fascinating link between the poison used and the very existence of reserves such as Tutanning, and why it is not a hazard to wildlife. The poison is known as 1080 or sodium fluoroacetate and is widely used for poisoning rabbits and dingoes. The same poison, in the form of fluoroacetic acid, is contained in some native plants of the pea family, as mentioned in the last chapter, and sheep are frequently poisoned by eating the plants. In some wheat-belt areas these plants were so abundant that farmers fenced off parts of their farms to keep the sheep out until they could get around to removing the poison bushes. Tutanning was overgrown with box poison, which had still not been cleared by the time it was recognised that there was a desperate need for conservation reserves in the wheat-belt to preserve remnants of the original flora and fauna. That is how the reserve came into being.

The same poison can be used to help preserve the wildlife without fear of killing native species because the wildlife has had time to evolve resistance to it over thousands of years. It has been found that woylies and possums can eat large quantities without being poisoned, and it has even been suggested that bronze-wing pigeons can be so poisonous that they can kill foxes which eat them. It is only the recent immigrants which are susceptible, so poison can be laid without any fear of decimating the native wildlife. A remarkable corollary to this detective work is that it has resolved a dispute on the origin of the grey kangaroo: did it evolve in eastern Australia and spread west or evolve in the west and spread east? The poison plants are not found outside Western Australia, but it has been found that the grey kangaroos in New South Wales are resistant to fluoroacetic acid, so it seems likely that they evolved here and spread east, carrying the genetic resistance with them.

Another conservation problem is caused by the kangaroos themselves, because they are the only species which can exploit farmland. They go out into the paddocks and graze the grass and crops, returning to the bushland reserves to sleep during the day. This means that they have ample food and can build up into such large populations that they put too much pressure on the reserves. The result is that the vegetation becomes so altered that the other native mammals, such as the bandicoots and brush wallabies, have no food and nowhere to hide because they cannot make use of the paddocks.

Preservation of these small relics of the original diversity of the natural countryside becomes an increasingly costly exercise, particularly because the more we know about it, the more we realise how much we have to intervene with management procedures to reduce the rate of change. One wonders whether sufficient funds will be available when most reserves get to the same sort of stage as Kings Park, where massive management is required to preserve the identity of the bushland.

Looking at these wheat-belt reserves, one is soon impressed by the incredible diversity in the flora and vegetation types varying according to the topography and soils. The most fascinating areas are the heathlands, which in some ways resemble English heaths. They are usually on light, quickly draining soils and have a vegetation cover of low, woody shrubs. The English heaths have largely survived until recently because the soil is so poor that they could not be cultivated. They became commons where parishioners could graze their stock, but this practice has now become history and most commons have been ploughed up with modern agriculture, have had nuclear power stations built on them or have been swallowed up by Forestry Commission plantations. The surviving areas are reverting to woodland in the absence of grazing. It is interesting that the English heaths are not a natural phenomenon; they were created by early agriculture — by Neolithic and Bronze Age people between about 6,000 years ago and the Roman conquest. The light soil areas were the easiest to clear and plant crops in, but the poor nature of the soil meant that it had to be a shifting agriculture, much like that practised in tropical rainforest. Eventually, the soil became so leached that it could not be cropped at all; in fact, many heaths developed an extraordinary soil structure as the iron in the sand was leached deep into the soil and was deposited as an impervious layer. Areas with this structure became waterlogged in winter and arid in summer.

Our heathland has no agricultural origins, but one must remember that it has evolved within the 40,000 years or so of Mesolithic land management. Frequent burning on poor, quickly draining soils may have a very similar effect to agriculture, mobilising the soil nutrients and allowing them to leach out with following rains.

It would be interesting to glimpse into the future of the wheat-belt. One hopes our land managers will prevent it from becoming a desert of shifting sands like the land which gave birth to agriculture in the Middle East. But its future does not look secure, because people tend to assume that modern agriculture can grow regular crops on any soil, even though we have such a short experience of it on the wheat-belt. Other parts of the globe have had longer experience, such as in western New South Wales which has severe erosion problems, while the erosion problems in the United States and South Africa can be appalling. When I first came here I was surprised not to see dust storms and gully erosion channels, but I was forgetting how recent the land clearance had been here. Since then I have been watching the gullies grow, as the last vestiges of deep roots and binding humus disappear from the soils. The soils have now become almost a dead chemical environment, compacted in places by heavy machinery. One of the well-known consequences has been the mobilisation of the salt in the soil. Instead of staying low down in the soil profile, held there by deep-rooted native vegetation, it has percolated nearer the surface, pouring out of the soil in winter-wet areas and turning them into salt deserts and salt lakes. This is one of the fates of wheat-belt agriculture. Other areas may succumb to sheet-wind-, or gully-erosion, or to a similar sort of leaching process to that in England, perhaps turning some soils into calcrete or an impervious iron layer.

One of the arguments for retaining natural bushland may be that it holds the diversity of plants, which can be used in the future to revegetate unusable agricultural land. If this is done in time, it may be possible to prevent the formation of the mobile desert sands characteristic of the Middle East. The value of surviving salt-tolerant species is already being exploited to revegetate badly salted land. Heathland plants may be the saving grace of highly leached light soil areas where wind erosion becomes a serious problem.

In England it was the ice-age tundra vegetation which came to the rescue of abandoned farmland, colonising the heaths and downland and adapting well to more temperate weather conditions, building up over thousands of years into complex man-made ecosystems. Research workers in America have set up a whole branch of ecology around this process as it is occurring in that country: it is the ecology of "old fields", which are abandoned farmlands. One study recently compared old-field invertebrates with those in an English pasture, and found that the American area had a very poor fauna, struggling to survive in the pasture made up of exotic weeds. There were no native plants in the area and there had not been time for the invertebrates to adapt to the new conditions. They presumably need a long time, perhaps thousands of years, to become adapted like the ones in England. Native species in Australia are even less well adapted to invading farmland due to the gulf between the alien plants and native plants being very much greater than between North America and Europe, which were all part of one land mass at the time when Neolithic agriculture was developing. These invertebrates are essential in the process of reconstructing the soil, and so in Australia it is particularly important to use native plants which already have their own invertebrate fauna when reclaiming unusable farmland.

Preventing the formation of an intractable desert is a costly process, particularly when farmers are falling into debt and are unable to afford any reclamation work. Fortunately, attitudes evolve with time, and there is an increasing shift towards reclamation work and soil conservation being seen as integral parts of farming, instead of being an additional expense imposed by government regulations. There is also a realisation that drought-relief measures tend to be counterproductive, just like food provision in famine relief; they merely prolong the cause of the malady, making the final solution far worse. There are also signs that many people are moving away from the notion that the land is there to be exploited solely for profit, particularly in those areas where farmers barely make a living. A realisation is coming that the farmers are there because that is their chosen lifestyle rather than it being a ticket to wealth. Many would do better to sell up and move their capital into something else if profit alone were the motive for living on the land.

I hope to see this evolutionary process gain strength, so that people on the land begin to regard themselves as its guardians, carefully managing it for the future. Many may be city people opting out of the rat-race and developing the land into country estates. They may even have the funds to employ the most up-to-date knowledge to re-create bushland over degraded uneconomic farmland. The need for this change is desperate if the projections about the greenhouse effect are true. With a hotter and drier climate, farming will become uneconomic over a much larger area, with more regular and severe droughts. (It has taken a long time for people to realise that droughts are a recurring feature of the climate and reliable rainfall is the exception, and that farming uses up the soil almost as if it were being mined.) This will bring in serious soil erosion to areas with unvegetated, structureless soils, grazed bare by stock. The Western Australian dustbowl may start with red clouds sweeping over Perth, much as they have done over Melbourne recently, particularly on the passage of a cyclone. Cyclonic rains on these impervious compacted soils could bring about an unmitigated disaster, with the massive run-off reaching Perth and causing the Swan River to flood the city.

Do we have long enough to evolve a sensible land management, or is it going to be forced on us when it is too late? The climatic change may already be in motion, yet it may take forty years for trees to develop deep, strong-rooting systems, and heathland bushes are notoriously slow growing. By the time the drought comes, it may not be possible to revegetate the worst affected land.

As one travels east it is a pleasant break to call in at Wave Rock. This is one of many granite tors within the wheat-belt, which are ideal for water catchment. Even light rain will run off the rock and collect in especially constructed dams. This water soaking into the base over thousands of years has been responsible for weathering the rock more rapidly to produce an undercut, wave-like cliff. Similar, but usually smaller, undercuts are commonly found around granite tors.

With this relatively certain supply of water, many plants and animals have become adapted to living around granite rocks. There are usually plenty of frogs, especially the banjo frog, which breeds in pools formed at the base. The males make a ringing "plonk" call while partly submerged in the water, sounding like the plucking of a banjo string. This is one of the few species benefiting from agriculture — it found farm dams very similar to its normal breeding ponds and quickly spread from its natural habitats, eventually finding its way to Perth. Other frogs have not been so lucky, like the spotted frog (*Heleioporus albopunctatus*) which burrows in clay in low-lying areas and calls when the autumn rains are due. Females come into the burrows and lay their eggs, the male staying behind until water floods the burrow, and releases the tadpoles. Most of these sites have now become saltpans, and the frogs have largely died out of the wheat-belt.

Sitting on the rock and watching a wedge-tailed eagle wheeling over the shimmering paddocks, I thought of the very different view the original people would have seen. The bushland would not have experienced some of the climatic extremes of today, because living bushland vegetation increases humidity and encourages more rainfall, it also shields the soil from extreme temperatures and drying winds. One wonders how much local climatic change is due to land clearance, and how much this has affected the rate of soil erosion.

Wave Rock near Hyden. This is one of many granite outcrops in the wheat-belt. The wave-like shape is the result of deep weathering at the edge of the rock. Aboriginal rock paintings have been found in the area.

4 The Goldfields: Pastoral Degradation

As I continued east through the wheat-belt, I progressively saw more remnants of the orginal vegetation at the roadside, especially patches of heathland with an abundance of grevilleas, hakeas, dryandras and verticordias. The flame grevilleas are particularly attractive, with their branches swept into artistic brushstrokes as if blown by the wind, and are covered in orange flowers stretched high into the air for honeyeaters to pollinate. In places, the strange mottlecah spread their whitish glaucous leaves from sprawling stems covered in huge gumnuts and scattered passionvine-like flowers. This is a kind of eucalypt and has the largest flowers of all Australian gum trees. Many of the trees and shrubs growing on the heathland have narrow, silvery, pine-like leaves to cope with the drying winds and unrelenting sunshine, especially the casuarinas, hakeas, grevilleas and leptomerias (a parasitic bush with small edible fruits, related to the sandalwood and quondong.) There are even native cypress pines (*Callitris*) which are well adapted to growing in this habitat.

After Southern Cross, I came to Yellowdine and drove through some of the eucalyptus forest which used to clothe most of the wheat-belt. Many of the trees had wonderful canopies looking like tiers of umbrellas. I was struck by the amount of work that the early settlers had to do to clear the land, which was mainly done by axe and burning in those days. Large trees were killed by ringbarking and some can still be seen in land cleared during the earlier days. However, bulldozers were used in more modern times and nothing remains in these areas to indicate what the land used to look like.

Walking through the mallee forest near Yellowdine, I nearly trod on a pair of nightjars resting invisibly camouflaged on the forest floor amongst piles of mallee bark. In this dry climate nothing rots, and the bark is so packed with tannins that even the toughest termites and beetles cannot eat it; it collects on the forest floor, like the blanket of pine needles in northern pine forests, shutting out the ground vegetation. Orchids with unusual flowers, including greenhoods and the ant orchid, occasionally push their way through the bark, and the bleached shells of a surprisingly large snail for this arid country, punctuate the ground. But even in this woodland, signs of human activity abound, with plastic survey tapes everywhere, flapping in the breeze. They serve to remind one of why the woodland was preserved in the first place: to provide pit-props and firewood for the goldminers.

Nearby I came to a hill made entirely of quartz and mica, although half of the hill had gone in goldmining activity. I sat on a sparkling stone and looked through the mallee to a salt lake and a granite hill on the other side. I could almost see the hoards of people trekking past in the days of the gold rush, making their way under incredible hardships from Perth to Kalgoorlie, pushing all their goods on a wheelbarrow. It seems as if people will put up with almost anything if they have the chance of getting rich. This reminded me of the people I had seen years ago feverishly digging holes in the rain-soaked forests of Guiana in South America, looking for diamonds. Most could not find enough to keep themselves going and became virtual slaves to the merchants, and those who did make a find were back digging in the mires in a few months, having spent all their wealth in Rio de Janeiro.

It is a strange world where there is a huge industry around this relatively useless metal, simply because long ago it acquired an abstract quality through being used as a medium of exchange. All the gold in the world could go tomorrow with little effect, yet we guard it with much greater care than the living environment on which the whole human race depends. The only value we appear to give to the living environment relates to how much pecuniary wealth can be extracted from it, whether in the form of gold, soil or woodchips. The Midas legend has a message, but few are listening.

As a biologist, rather than a classics scholar, I drifted into thinking about lemmings and how the human race has got into part of a lemming cycle. The cycle goes something like this: it starts with a wealth of overgrown habitat suitable for colonisation and with few predators. The few pioneer lemmings chew into the landscape and breed without restraint, and the young do not have to move far to set up new homes and start families. The grass supports the snow in winter, forming a protective blanket to keep out the cold and the predators. The next year things are better: with an extended community and plenty of food, the whole area is chewed and trampled into lemming habitat. But as the rapid breeding continues, things are not looking as good by the end of the year. The abundance of prey has encouraged predators to build up, and the lemmings find it harder to hide because they have eaten most of their protective vegetation cover. The third year is a disaster. They eat the rest of the vegetation cover and the population crashes, some move great distances trying to find new homes, while those staying behind have a very hard winter with no vegetation to keep the snow off the ground. It takes another year for the vegetation to recover, getting ready for the next cycle.

The human race has not been through cycles such as this, except on a local scale, because each new level of technology has allowed for further population growth, and we are still marching into new uncolonised global habitat. It is only in our generation or the next that for the first time there will be no unexploited global habitat left. This is when a new technology fundamentally different from the present will have to be developed, if we are to avoid a biological solution such as that experienced by the lemmings each time their population crashes.

The problem with the lemmings is that each individual is not directly accountable for preserving its habitat — it does not live long enough to reap the consequences of its own habitat-destroying activities. Their problem arises because they live in a simple, lemming-dominated environment lacking the complexity of warmer climates, where populations are automatically controlled by diverse predators, competitors, pathogens, etc. The same is true for people, although we live much longer than lemmings; it is only two or three generations down the track that are going to reap the devastating consequences of our mismanagement of the global habitat, now totally dominated and simplified by human activity. Unless, of course, a nuclear winter arrives first and sends the human race down the dinosaur track earlier.

Our farmers are those closest to reaping the consequences of land mismanagement. They have a direct interest in maintaining productivity, but lack of scientific data and governmental haste for rapid economic development have meant that the farmers have become trapped in the system. For instance, the problem of salt was not appreciated until the 1950s and not acted on until the 1980s, when it could no longer be ignored, and the problems of drought, salt and soil erosion meant that farmers were managing properties which are not economically viable in the long term. The farmers cannot afford reconstruction work or taking areas out of production to stop the spread of salt, let alone pay finance houses when they fall into debt. Meanwhile, the gullies are getting deeper. Farming is relatively young here, so land managers should see other dry-land farming areas in longer-settled countries to see the sort of gullies and soil erosion problems the next generation of farmers is going to have to cope with.

If our farmers find it hard to manage their land so that productivity is sustainable for several generations, what hope is there that finance houses and large public companies, based in London, New York and Tokyo, will fare any better and successfully manage the world's natural resources? Their only real consideration is the computer print-out of profits at the end of the year and, being able to rapidly switch their operations, they have little need to base their future on sustainable production. This is particularly worrying when they are effectively responsible for the future of tropical rainforests and ocean fisheries. The companies certainly do not have much accountability; they do not go broke when the forests are cleared out, but move on investing elsewhere. It is only the local inhabitants who are to go down the spiral of land degradation and poverty following forest clearance. We have to accept that it is not the peasants of the Third World who are at the forefront of environmental destruction; it is the very rich, the decision-makers, the bankers, governments and multinational companies.

At the other end of the spectrum, who is going to stop famine-stricken peoples scratching the last vestiges of vegetation from the ground, when the problem resides in Western technology arriving before birth control and a Westernised education? These peoples are directly accountable for their actions, but, like the lemmings, day-to-day survival takes precedence over tomorrow's environment. Is this the end point for the global society, when Western technology can no longer support world population growth? It will certainly happen if Western civilisation is too slow in heeding the warnings of overconsumption and over-exploitation based on present technology.

The biological solution is very sudden and dramatic, and if climatic change is to occur, it is likely to upset the precarious balance sooner rather than later. The spectre of shortfalls in the supply of grain is already becoming more real every year. Famine is one biological solution, a myxomatosis-like disease is another. AIDS already looks as if it may buy time for some countries by temporarily reversing population growth. If it can mutate into a more readily transmissible form, as plague and syphilis did (see my *Evolution in the Outback*, 1987), then it could become the myxomatosis-factor.

The problem with our financial system is the lack of any direct form of accountability. The main driving force in the environmental sphere is to convert what is there, both rapidly and efficiently, into pecuniary wealth — the Midas Touch. Yet the more wealth is created, the more our monetary system seems to become based on abstract factors. It is fast becoming merely numbers in computers that are far removed from any form of accountability; the figures do not even really measure a return for labour or possessions any more. Money based on primary production seems to be manipulated on a world scale, flashing from computer to computer, making financial killings for some, while devaluing the financial resources of the majority. Those working on the land are powerless to do anything about it and may be quite unaware of what is going on, apart from the fact that tractors cost more and they get less for their crops. But the result is that they have to mine their soil and natural resources ever faster to make a living. What is needed is a value-system which reflects the real long-term costs of materials and does not deposit the natural wealth of the land in the form of lifeless gold bars languishing at Fort Knox, or as arsenals of lethal weapons, or as computer figures to be wiped clean at the next stock-market crash.

Most of the people in the world now live in cities and have little more contact with environmental accountability than the price of a hamburger or fresh water, and their experience of wildlife extends little further than their local pests or what they see on television. In fact few of us are even aware of the origins of most of the materials we use, and we are growing less aware as the world population becomes more urbanised and city-born. This makes it difficult to change our system so that the environment can be protected. Ideally, there should be different costs ascribed to things according to their environmental impacts. For example, electricity generated from hydro schemes flooding natural forest or from fossil fuel should be costed differently from that produced by solar generation. Paper from natural forest should be far more expensive than that from plantations or straw. Farmed fish should be cheaper than ocean-caught fish, and so on.

Many items such as fur and ivory should be made non-purchasable to reduce the slaughter of wild animals. But even this cannot save the rhino, which is almost guaranteed to become extinct in the wild due to the black-market value placed on its horns. Action to save these animals, like whales, can become popular movements, but it is much harder to change huge industries based on environmentally damaging activity, because they are so entrenched in our society. Because they are so widespread they have a much more damaging effect on the environment than the removal of the last few specimens of the dodo or rhino. Action is desperately needed in the paper and forest-products area to safeguard surviving forested areas.

International pressure is mounting, but it is unlikely to do more than save a few patches of forest as long as native forest timber is a commodity which can be exchanged for gold. The only hope lies in finding cheaper alternatives, such as using the vast amounts of straw and agricultural waste from sugar cane, which are normally burnt, or replacing the daily paper with an electronic device which can display newspapers from something such as microfilm in an acceptable way. This would indeed deserve a Nobel Prize, as long as the new medium could be enforced, and newspapers replaced all over the globe.

Nearer to home, the progressive destruction of rangelands by grazing animals has a huge sheep and beef industry centred on it. As a means of converting solar energy into a usable product, sheep being used to produce wool must be one of the world's most inefficient and environmentally damaging forms of land usage. If this cost were reflected in the price of wool, it would probably soon disappear in favour of harder-wearing artificial fibres (although they have their own environmental costs in terms of air pollution from the petrochemical industry).

This raises another issue — durability. Much of the human economy is based on inbuilt obsolescence. If things did not break down or wear out after a short time, industries would grind to a halt, or so economic theory tells us. Consequently, we even have a fashion industry which seems to be based on creating artificial obsolescence to speed up the process. I was reminded of the film *The Man in the White Suit*, about a material which had been invented that was supposedly indestructible. The clothing and fibre industry was facing financial ruin, but fortunately the day was saved by the material disintegrating.

Walking back to the car I found that my shoes had developed a thicker sole — the disturbance of gold mining had opened the ground to alien weeds and I was propped up on doublegees stuck into the soles of my shoes (the name comes from the Africaans word *dubbeltjie*). These are the seeds of a plant belonging to the dock family which are designed to be dispersed by sticking into the feet of heavy-footed animals in South Africa. This is nothing new for our native kangaroos, because they already had to cope with caltrop, which probably evolved its seeds when there were large diprotodons and megornithid flightless birds in Australia before the last ice age.

Driving on towards Kalgoorlie, I found the countryside was a real relief from the devastation of the wheat-belt. There were still hundreds of kilometres of wooded mallee country and heathland, enough for unobservant people flying over the continent to suggest that only small parts of the Australian ecosystem have been destroyed. However, the relentless grazing force of millions of cattle, sheep and goats is ever present in pastoral areas, eating further and further into the vegetation. The change is largely imperceptible — a dying mallee is replaced by a thorn bush here, a perennial shrub is replaced by annual weeds there. One may only be made aware of the change by reading early descriptions, such as of grassy banks and bluebush around lakes now bare or overgrown with saltbush.

The rocks underlying the area are remarkable, not only for their gold, but also for what they tell us about the history of the Earth. One cannot help being impressed by the age of the landscape; it is so old that few features are visible. The effects of weathering have reduced hills and mountains to a flat terrain, deeply weathered even below ground level. This has made life difficult for field geologists because few rocks are visible for them to identify the geological strata, and weathering has greatly altered the original rock material, even when drilling deep into the earth. The goldfields are on an area known as the Yilgarn Block, made up of rocks which are mainly older than 2,500 million years. It is one of the oldest and least altered blocks of rock on the planet, having remained much the same without mountain-building actions since it was being formed. Some believe that this relatively stable period is near an end; they suggest the Meckering earthquake was the start of a new rift valley which will open out to make a new inland sea, cutting the south-west off from the rest of Australia.

The presence of gold tells us a surprising amount about the land when it was being formed. We know, for instance, that the surface was at least five kilometres above the present level. Research on the deposition of gold has found that it is formed in a hydrothermal process, that is by hot springs. The gold is held in a relatively low concentration in the hard greenstone rocks characteristic of the region. These rocks were produced as liquid magma (large masses of lava), and as they cooled, water within the rock and coming from other strata was heated and rose in hot springs, much like those at Rotorua or in Yellowstone Park. This water would be at high temperatures and pressure because it was deep in the earth at the time, and under these conditions gold and other minerals, such as silica, become soluble in the presence of carbon dioxide and sulphur. Thus, the water running through fissures in the greenstone leached out silica and gold and carried them upwards. The pressure decreased as it rose until it dropped too low for gold to be soluble, and it became deposited, with silica in the form of quartz later filling up the fissures in the rock. Tiny droplets of the liquid remain in the quartz today, telling mineralogists that it was indeed this method of deposition, that can only occur in relatively pure carbonated water, and not the salt water mechanism found at Boddington. The water pressure required to stay liquid at the temperature that gold becomes soluble (250–350°C) only occurs at depths of five to ten kilometres, so that is why it is known how much rock has been eroded away from the goldfields.

It is strange that most of the world's gold deposits occur from similar mechanisms in rocks of about the same age. Something unusual was happening about 2,700 million years ago which led to gold deposition. Mineral deposits in rocks of this age are traditionally thought to have come from some form of chemical deposition, because the rocks are older than those of the Proterozoic, when the first fossils were found. However, it is now known that life was present much earlier than this, being already complex 3,500 million years ago. It is now becoming accepted that the vast tracts of iron ore laid down between 2,500 and 1,800 million years ago were mediated by the activity of bacteria in shallow lakes. Kanowna has some wonderful fossil stromatolites which were built by bacteria living at the time. It seems strange that gold should be concentrated in this period of time if there was not some unknown factor involved. It is thought that the gold might have come from rocks containing lamprophyres as much as 150 kilometres below the surface, but how did it get into the greenstone dolerite? Was it through an asteroid hitting the earth, which left the minute spherules and concentrations of iridium metal in the greenstones of Australia and South Africa (and, incidentally, the signs of huge tidal waves known as tsunami), or was there some gold-concentrating mechanism during the previous 1,000 million years? I wonder whether bacteria-like organisms were involved, because it is known that living organisms preferred much hotter conditions then than they do today. Some, like *Bacillus cereus*, still like heavy metals and can be used in gold prospecting.

We glibly talk about bacteria as if they were a single kind of organism, but in reality the differences between different groups of bacteria are greater than between any other two sets of organisms — plants, animals, fungi, whatever — because they have been evolving ever since life appeared on the planet, not just in the last few hundred million years. Aerobic species are clearly very advanced, because they can survive in oxygen, which first appeared in the atmosphere about 1,800 million years ago. The anaerobic species dominated the globe prior to this. Nowadays we find them producing methane at the bottom of ponds, in iron-stained deposits in ditches and in coloured patches in hot springs or depositing sulphides around smokers at the bottom of oceans, and they have even been found deep in the earth in oil fields. They have been found to concentrate gold and other minerals around hot springs, where they thrive in temperature extremes well above those that other forms of life can tolerate. Could they in some way have played a part in bringing gold into the rocks?

Many oil deposits have similarly been a mystery, but bacteria are increasingly being implicated in their formation, first of all in forming methane gas and then in converting it into oil. At least 10,000 million tons of the gas lurk on the floor of oceans in the form of methane hydrate, and more carbon is held in these gas deposits than in all the world's coalfields put together. Some fear that rising ocean temperatures will release the gas into the atmosphere, where it will accelerate the greenhouse effect. One wonders how much is needed to start a runaway greenhouse effect like the one on the planet Venus (which is hot enough to release the vast quantities of CO_2 held in terrestrial limestone).

The goldfields have interesting relics of past oceans, because some of the greenstone rock was clearly deposited underwater. Pillow-shaped chunks of lava are formed by liquid rock being forced into cold water, where it quickly develops a solid skin. Then, as pressure mounts inside, it cracks and another pillow is released and so on, depositing layers of what is known as pillow-lava. Divers have filmed the process where lavas are being deposited in the mid-ocean rises. These underwater mountain chains are fascinating places which explain many mineral deposits in the goldfields. "Smokers" have been found which are underwater geysers or hot springs pushing out vast quantities of minerals in the water, blackened by the metal sulphides they contain. Bacteria swarm around the smokers, even though the water emerging may be as high as 300°C due to the water pressure, and form the basis of a complex food chain which supports strange animals not seen before. They include worms belonging to new phyla (equivalent in zoological circles to finding vertebrates for the first time). The ocean floor around the smokers collects deposits of metal sulphides rich in nickel and manganese, often forming spherical nodules. These nodules are frequently found in fine-grained rocks formed on ocean floors, especially clays and shales. Mining companies have been investigating methods of trawling these nodules from the ocean floor. Other traces of the smokers can be found in rocks which have been chemically altered by the passage of hot water. Dolerites and other basic rocks have had their minerals, especially feldspars, hydrolysed into substances such as talc.

It is interesting that evidence is mounting that life is more likely to have originated in this sort of environment than near the surface of shallow seas, which is the more accepted venue. Clays possess remarkable chemical properties which would favour the formation of complex molecules based on silicon, and the environment around a smoker would provide ample heat and chemical energy to foster the evolution of self-replicating molecules which only later changed to the carbon-based DNA molecules of life as we know it. The fact that life appeared on earth so soon after its formation suggests that it must have its origins in conditions which would destroy most present-day organisms — unless it arrived from space instead. The earth was still hot, and the atmosphere and water full of poisonous gases and acids: hydrogen sulphide, methane, sulphuric acid, nitric acid, etc. One wonders how deep in the earth these early processes occurred. Could some of the original processes still be occurring deep down in the smokers where the rocks are too hot for us to handle?

Gold has recently been found in the Pacific rim which is of much more recent origin than most of the previously known gold deposits. This discovery has led to a modern goldrush which is centered on what were hot spring areas only 5 million years ago. The age of these recent deposits was an interesting time for the planet: it was active with many mountain ranges being formed, such as the Himalayas and New Guinean Highlands, while Indonesia was pushed up out of the ocean. It was also the time when the great apes were setting the scene for the origin of the human race. Scientists are studying the gold-rich hot muds of New Zealand to see if they can throw any light on this gold deposition process.

The countryside around Kalgoorlie takes on the look of a lunar landscape, because it has been the scene of so much mining and bulldozer-prospecting activity. The vegetation is greatly altered, but even so, some plants can still be used by prospectors for finding nickel and iron deposits, in the same way that jarrah can be used to indicate bauxite. The rich mineralisation of the goldfields has partly been the reason for the enormous variety of mallee trees found there; in fact, a large proportion of the world's species of eucalypts are found growing within a few hundred kilometres of Kalgoorlie. The complex mineralisation of the area has meant that local soil conditions vary so much that trees have evolved local adaptations to grow successfully and, in the course of time, have become separate species.

It is interesting to compare farming and the pastoral industry with mining in terms of their effects on the environment. Farming totally removes the ecosystem over vast tracts of land, while the pastoral industry progressively degrades and changes much of the remainder. Actual mining occurs only over a minute area in comparison. However, it does have other environmental problems. Mineralised areas are often the only bits of land left relatively untouched by the pastoral and farming industries, and the unusual soils of mineral deposits often develop unique floras and faunas, such as the goldfields gum trees, which are destroyed by mining activity. But the main damaging effects are related to factors peripheral to mining: for instance, little regard was given to native vegetation when prospecting work was conducted, which has meant that most of arid Australia is now patterned with the traces of mineral prospecting activity, such as seismic lines, which have brought modern disturbance to even the remotest areas. The mining activity itself, even if only a small operation, will bring disturbance, pests and weeds into the heart of otherwise relatively pristine areas. These pests and weeds accelerate the process of degradation and change in the surrounding countryside well away from the small area subject to mining activity, and make it less likely that areas of natural ecosystem will survive long enough for the species to adapt to modern conditions.

It is interesting that little thought ever seems to be given to the fact that mining is a one-off operation. Minerals will not grow in the ground again, like forests. The energy crisis in the 1970s slowed the use of oil because it was said that it was going to run out. We still know that it is going to run out, but we are now using oil faster than ever. The crisis was clearly

Flame grevillea. A common shrub up to 6 m tall which grows on sandy heaths especially in the eastern wheat-belt. Its pine-like leaves are an adaptation to the hot dry climate.

Pink spike hakea. A shrub which grows on gravel soils between Mullewa and Southern Cross. It grows up to 7 m tall with attractive spikes of pink or red flowers from July to September.

Quondong tree with fruit. These trees are closely related to the sandalwood and have attractive red fruit containing a large nut. The fruit is eaten by emus which use the nuts as gizzard stones and distribute them in their dropping. The tree is a semi-parasite like mistletoe, attaching its roots to those of neighbouring trees and shrubs.

Gum trees near Kalgoorlie. About half of the known species of gum tree grow within a few hundred kilometres of Kalgoorlie. Many have attractive growth forms like these, with new canopies growing above old ones to give a tiered umbrella effect.

Quartz hill. Hills such as these excite prospectors, because they may contain gold. Gold is associated with quartz because the two materials become soluble in high-pressure hot water, deep in the earth. As the water rises, pressure decreases until the two are deposited together in cracks in the rock to form quarts veins. The mauve-flowered rock isotome is very interesting because the plants are isolated on each rocky outcrop, and each population has a different genetic structure.

Pastoral land with windmill. Sheep come to drink near mills and so tend to graze more heavily in these areas. The effects of this grazing become obvious with the removal of most shrubs from the area. Grazing effects are less obvious away from the mills, but considerable change occurs in the vegetation over long periods of time, altering the ecology of pastoral areas.

more a political one over the pricing of oil and a revolt against the old form of colonialism. Present economic and political realities seem to be far more important than conserving oil for the future. Like wool and timber, there is such a huge industry around oil that alternatives such as solar power are seen as a threat instead of a way out of our problems. We tend to forget that we are in a fossil fuel and mineral era which will definitely come to an end in the foreseeable future. As with the forests and natural environment, one is forced to ask: do all mineral resources have to go before mining stops or should we conserve at least some for the future? It may be that when alternative technologies have been developed, fossil minerals may have some important value that we do not appreciate at present. At one time Australia tried to conserve strategic minerals, such as iron ore and uranium, and this policy had to be reversed before iron ore could be exported from the Pilbara. This policy now seems to have been superseded by a short-term economic one: Sell it now while we know we can get some money for it, and to hell with the future. Gold could well be more valuable if it were left in the ground rather than languishing in state coffers.

Gold is such a heavy, inert metal that one wonders what has happened to the tons of metal deposited, as the kilometres of rock were washed away from the land surface. Some has been found washed into old river systems as alluvial deposits, especially at Cue, and a few heavy nuggets have been found lying on the surface. The rest has gone, possibly blown away in the dust which contributed to the gold mineralisation at Boddington and lead in Antarctic ice, or carried in clays to salt lakes, where it dissolved in salt water and was carried out to sea. The salt lakes are interesting repositories of minerals in the goldfields; much of the calcium is also carried into the lakes and may be deposited as large crystals of gypsum (calcium sulphate) in the clay.

Lake Yindarlgooda, near Kalgoorlie, has collected another very interesting deposit of marble-like beads, which have been rolled there by water flowing over the surrounding catchment area. It is made up of light-weight black-glass tektites which are easily carried by flowing water. They come from a very violent geological event which took place about 700,000 years ago. It may have been volcanic, but more likely was caused by a comet or asteroid striking the Earth somewhere south of Australia. The force of the strike vaporised rock and showered southern Australia with these black glass beads. Over 80,000 have been found in the lake bed, mainly rather abraded on the surface, having been rolled along in stream beds.

The surface of the globe is like an enormous library telling us about the history of the Earth and the Universe, written for any civilisation that has the technology to read it and the intelligence to look after it. The Aborigines used a few of the tektites for making into spearheads. Had they prized them as much as we prize gold, we would have little chance of knowing much about the event 700,000 years ago when they were formed.

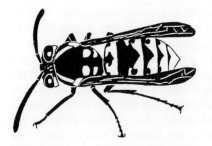

European Wasp *(Vespula germanica)*. Quarantine regulations exist to try and stop pest species lke this wasp entering and becoming established in Western Australia. This species probably came in crates shipped from Victoria, Tasmania or New Zealand and has been in Perth for about 15 years. The wasp is likely to become a costly pest, because the winters are not cold enough to kill the nests which become enormous, and there are no natural enemies to control its numbers.

5 The Nullarbor: New Species, New Invaders

Heading east from Norseman, I soon passed the Quarantine Station where vehicles coming from Eastern Australia are searched. The check is necessary to try and prevent pests and weeds which are not yet established there from being carried into Western Australia. These include European wasps, skeleton weed, sparrows, starlings, etc. One of the main reasons for the station was to stop the Queensland fruit-fly from entering the state, but it was too easy for travellers by air, rail or car to bring untreated fruit with them, and so the fly was found to be infesting Perth in 1989. Established European wasps' nests and annual skeleton weed infestations have also been found, and it is only a matter of time before all of these and the other species are added to the flora and fauna of Western Australia.

At this point, like many travellers, I thought that the Nullarbor was just around the corner. But after many hundreds of kilometres of mainly mallee country, I stopped to look at the vegetation map and found that the Eyre Highway travels too near to the coast, and almost entirely misses the Nullarbor Plain, apart from a short section in South Australia. Rail travellers, however, get a good view of the treeless plain, providing they are lucky enough to pass through the area during daylight hours.

I stopped for a while on the Hampton Tablelands near Cocklebiddy where there were patches of vegetation similar to that on the Nullarbor — a low scrub of mainly bluebush (*Maireana*, previously known as *Kochia*) which belongs to the spinach family (Chenopodiaceae). This bush has largely been eaten out of overgrazed pastoral areas in the north of Australia by cattle and sheep. It has silvery hairs on its leaves which reflect the light, protecting the plant from intense sunlight and drying winds. It is strange that plants in the Australian desert, which is an old one compared to others such as the Sonora in Mexico, have not developed the succulent (water-storing) characteristics like those found in the cacti. The bluebush is one of the few which have semi-succulent leaves (others include saltbushes and pigface); it seems to do particularly well on alkaline, calcareous soils and where it is mildly saline. On the true Nullarbor Plain it is often the only bush visible as far as the eye can see.

The sun was high in the sky and the heat haze shimmering over the bluebush produced a mirage, reflecting distant mallee trees and prickly kurara shrubs. I could picture the problems Eyre faced in his journey from Adelaide to Esperance in this hot, waterless expanse. These conditions made the journey difficult for him, but it was no barrier to the desert people who had lived off the land in the area for generations. The human race does seem to have originally been a desert-adapted species.

On scanning the bush my eye was caught by a brilliant, almost luminous, red bird; it was a crimson chat. These birds are one of many which are well adapted to living in desert areas. It feeds on insects and breeds near salt lakes. It is odd to think that the existence of this species of bird was brought about by the Nullarbor being a barrier to species adapted to more humid environments. This barrier has had a remarkable effect on the Australian fauna in the last few hundred thousand years, because the climate has fluctuated with the ice ages, causing the Nullarbor to go through periods when it was wet enough for species to cross, interspersed with dry periods, much drier than at present. This process has been the root cause of generating a wide variety of new bird and mammal species.

With the chats it is thought that the coastal white-fronted chat was the original species, which now occurs all along the south coast and on both sides of the Nullarbor. It is thought that this bird only lived on the east side during dry periods, but in wet times it would cross to the west. On the return of dry conditions, the western population would become isolated from the eastern population and had to adapt to the local conditions as they became progressively drier. After a period of, say, 20,000 years, when wet conditions returned, the isolated birds in the west were no longer recognised as belonging to the same species by their eastern counterparts, because they had so changed their colour patterns, behaviour and genetic make-up. The eastern birds returned to colonise the wet coastal places, while the new arid-adapted species would follow drier conditions inland. In the course of time it would become desert-adapted, and spread throughout the Australian inland. This process happened at least twice, giving rise to the orange and crimson chats. Other chats were probably created by populations becoming isolated by a similar process across the tropical north of Australia. The last severe drought ended about 16,000 years ago, and the white-fronted chat would have returned to the west some time after this, certainly before 6,000 years ago when there was an unusually wet period.

The birds are particularly common on Rottnest Island, and in another 20,000 years time could evolve into yet another species. However, human interference with the biology of the world is becoming so intense that it is unlikely that any chats will survive the mass extinction, let alone evolve into new species. The previous worst mass extinction occurred about 245 million years ago when ice ages struck at the end of the Permian Era, and at least 90 per cent of the world's species became extinct. The human-generated mass extinction which is occurring now seems to be wiping species out at a rate unprecedented in the history of the globe, and on present trends may well result in 99 per cent of the world's species becoming extinct. This compares with only about 75 per cent when the dinosaurs became extinct.

The Nullarbor is remarkable for the number of caves found there. The plain is underlain by deep limestone which in the course of time has been dissolved away by rainfall and underground streams to form a labyrinth of caves. Many stories exist of vehicles disappearing, and people drilling through into vast caverns when sinking bores for water, and it is the location of the longest cave system known in the world. Caves near Cocklebiddy show plenty of signs of Aboriginal use, and when my son went down one of them with an Aboriginal leader they found stone implements and many ancient bones, which included the skull of the western barred bandicoot. This species used to occur right across Australia, but is now extinct on the mainland and only persists on Bernier and Dorre Islands in Shark Bay.

Caves often provide time capsules for palaeontologists and archaeologists, because they can show what lived in the area in the past, provide details of past weather patterns, and how people lived at the time. The Nullarbor caves have proved to be extremely valuable, because many have openings which act like pitfall traps. Unwary animals running across the plain suddenly fall to their death, and their bodies lie in the cavern out of reach of predators and scavengers to be preserved for posterity. The bones accumulate year after year to provide a detailed record of the fauna. One cave provided an almost perfect Tasmanian "wolf" or thylacine, mummified with its fur and all so that it looked as if it had only recently died. However, carbon-dating gave a different story — it died about 3,000 years ago. This is the largest recent marsupial carnivore, which became extinct on the mainland soon after the Aborigines acquired domestic dogs, probably through contact with people living in Indonesia. Some 10,000 years before this thylacine died, Bass Strait was flooded by the rising sea level caused by the ice caps melting. This isolated the people in Tasmania from the mainland, so that they never acquired dingoes, and the thylacine was able to survive there until the Europeans came with their guns and dogs. It took them only until 1933 to cause its extinction, although there is still a chance that it may persist in the wilderness areas of Tasmania.

When Eyre walked across the desert it was populated by a rich marsupial fauna. There was a wide variety of bandicoots, small wallabies, rat-kangaroos, together with unusual species like the marsupial mole and numbat. These were all desert-adapted species, living in an area which seemed to be least affected by European colonisation. Yet they are now nearly all either extinct, like the pig-footed bandicoot, or confined to offshore islands. Those remaining on the mainland are mostly living in areas well away from their preferred habitat, like the numbats at Dryandra and woylies in the jarrah forest near Manjimup. Recent research is showing how this mass-extinction has occurred, even though there has been little direct European influence on the vast Australian desert. One effect has been the loss of the Aboriginal population living in the desert. These people had a profound effect on the vegetation by burning it off in a mosaic of small burns. This activity increased the vegetation diversity and encouraged the mammalian fauna, because the animals were able to survive in nearby unburned areas from which they could colonise the burned sites as soon as there was enough regrowth. Without this Aboriginal management, the desert now grows for many years between burns, so that when a lightning strike or a careless person starts a fire, it burns uncontrollably over millions of hectares, incinerating or starving to death all the animals in its wake, and leaving no refuge areas.

The other major effect has been caused by introduced European mammals. During a wet period in the 1920s the Nullarbor became a green sward ideal for the European rabbit, which was best adapted to open, arid areas. It spread in from South Australia and boomed into enormous populations, closely followed by the European fox. When the drought returned, the rabbits migrated west seeking greener grass, and their numbers were so great that fence lines could not stop them, because they became piled high with bodies, and later arrivals were able to climb over. The remaining rabbits ate out the last remnants of vegetation before dying, leaving little cover for the remaining marsupials. The foxes did very well as long as the rabbits lasted, but they then experienced the drought themselves, and had to turn to native animals and to migrate west as well. They appeared in the Southwest in the 1930s, at about the same time as the woylies began to disappear in their strongholds near Dryandra.

It has been found that the desert marsupials can survive and breed in their old habitats as long as foxes are kept out. But foxes and rabbits prevent any general resurgence of native species, because rabbits persist in better pockets of vegetation, where they keep the vegetation cover down, and also maintain a residual fox population which soon catch any returning marsupials. Pastoralists also have an indirect effect through killing dingoes,

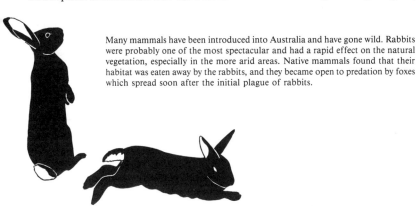

Many mammals have been introduced into Australia and have gone wild. Rabbits were probably one of the most spectacular and had a rapid effect on the natural vegetation, especially in the more arid areas. Native mammals found that their habitat was eaten away by the rabbits, and they became open to predation by foxes which spread soon after the initial plague of rabbits.

because these dogs are the only effective fox-predator. The final straw for the desert environment is the large animals which severely alter the environment by grazing and trampling. They include the pastoralists' cattle and sheep, and the many feral goats, donkeys, horses and camels which have no natural controls on their numbers.

The cave deposits and fossils around the world tell us that the loss of these desert marsupials is just the last catastrophic phase of a long history of extinction in the latter phases of the era of the great mammals. It is a mass extinction on the scale of that at the end of the dinosaurs, which is recorded in the rocks under the Nullarbor. At that time the Nullarbor was under the sea and marine life deposited its calcareous skeletons to form the deep layer of limestone. These layers can be seen in the cliffs along the Bight where there is a deep Cretaceous limestone, overlain by Eocene limestone which was deposited after the death of the dinosaurs. The rocks were deposited at a time when Australia was breaking away from Antarctica, and tipped slightly so that the sea came in over the Bight.

The continent was then covered with the temperate forests mentioned in Chapter 1, but as it moved north the climate became warmer and drier so that the forest began to give way to grasslands in the Nullarbor area. In Miocene times, about 15 million years ago, grazing mammals took advantage of the evolving grassy plains, and became larger and more numerous so that remaining woodlands were eaten away. This was the peak of mammalian evolution, when the world became populated with huge land mammals, thundering over the plains. Australia had its own huge mammals, ranging from giant kangaroos and rhinoceros-sized diprotodons, to lion-like predators such as thylacoleo, which were all marsupials. There were even giant flightless birds, especially the megornithids, looking very like bipedal, bird-like dinosaurs.

The end started with the arrival of the intelligent apes which began to spread over the globe during the onset of a new period of ice ages. The combination of fluctuating climates and intensified activity by an intelligent predator, particularly during the last 30,000 years, whittled away at the ecosystem of the great mammals until the majority became extinct. We are lucky enough to see the remnants still populating the globe, especially in Africa; although few are likely to survive in the wild for more than a couple of human generations on current projections.

I drove on towards the old Eyre Telegraph Station, south-east of Cocklebiddy, which is now used as a bird observatory by the Royal Australasian Ornithologists Union. The road suddenly came to a steep escarpment with a precipitous rocky track leading to the bottom. I left the car and walked to the edge to await the arrival of the four-wheel drive which was to take me to the observatory. I passed a mallee fowl's nest on the way. These extraordinary birds use sun-heated sand to incubate their eggs instead of sitting on them like most other birds. The males spend hours of the day tending the huge mound, checking on its temperature with a special organ on the neck, and raking sand on or off the mound as necessary. Females come and lay their eggs, leaving the male to do all the work. One of the extraordinary things about the bird is that when the young emerge, they are so well developed that they rush off into the bush and have nothing to do with the parents. They have in their brains at the moment of hatching all they need to know in order to live, build mounds and carry on the species. It is a source of wonder that the genetic code can transmit such a wealth of information, besides determining the structure and function of the body. Yet, when you think of it, even the minutest insect is fully programmed in its genes to carry out its life, which may need much more innate "knowledge" than that required by the young mallee fowl.

I walked on to sit on a limestone boulder overlooking the coastal plain. This massive inland cliff line is easy to see from the air when flying across Australia; it runs from Israelite Bay to near the South Australian border where it becomes an active sea-cliff again, stretching for hundreds of kilometres. The inland part demonstrates how recently the land has risen along this section of the Nullarbor. Not long ago the sea lashed at the base of this cliff, and the sandy coastal plain below was covered in marine life.

Looking down I could see the track going on in a straight line through tall mallees towards brilliant white sand-dunes in the distance. Near my feet I noticed what looked like a large ant scurrying over the ground and digging small pits in the sand. A closer look showed it to be a kind of wingless wasp known as a velvet ant. This reminded me of an exciting find which was made in mallee country somewhere between Esperance and Adelaide in the 1930s. It was *Nothomyrmecia* or the "dinosaur ant" which is the most primitive ant known. It was not known exactly where the animal was collected, and for years scientists tried to rediscover it. Eventually it turned up in mallee country in South Australia, similar to that near the Eyre Bird Observatory. The reason it was not found has much to do with its way of life. It has no visible nest, and only comes out at the dead of night, hunting individually. It probably represents an early stage in the evolution of ant societies, about 100 million years ago, when they were evolving from their ancestral wasps. This was during the time when dinosaurs were building up to their climax.

The interesting features of this ant are not so much to do with its anatomy, but more what it cannot do compared with modern ants: it cannot leave scent-blazed trails to find its way back to the nest or for other ants to follow; it cannot communicate the location of food to others; it has no division of labour, and does not have any different castes of worker. It persists by having a unique lifestyle, coming out when it is cold, and foraging individually, catching and stinging to death insects made torpid by the cold. It finds its way about by using the pattern of mallee branches silhouetted against the night sky.

These ants are somewhat like bulldog ants, which are at a more advanced stage in social evolution but still retain wasp-like characteristics. It is interesting to ponder the role of social evolution in shaping the biological world. It appears to open up whole new vistas of complexity. The herds of grazing mammals in Africa would not survive if it were not for a loose social structure which gives them protection from predators. This social structure allows them to exist, and so alter the whole ecology of the area, by grazing the veldt, removing woody plants and maintaining the grasslands.

The insect world is full of examples of loose social organisations, such as aphid colonies and processionary caterpillars, but it also possesses social organisations which far surpass any found in the mammals, and which in many respects are well in advance of our own. The peaks of complexity are achieved by the termites and ants, both of which evolved at about the same time. They have produced colonies which go far beyond individualism, having evolved complex structures which exert profound influences on the ecology of the land. Fortunately they did not appear suddenly, otherwise their success would have destroyed much of the globe's ecosystems, much as we are destroying them now. They evolved slowly within the world's ecosystems, moulding the evolution of plants and animals to accommodate the presence of these social insects. Strangely the termites have specialised in utilising dead plant material, so perform a very useful function, rarely damaging living plants, while the ants have specialised in predation, again helping plants by controlling damaging insects. Together they form the most important element in recycling energy in terrestrial ecosystems, termites eating more than grazing mammals, and ants more protein than carnivores.

One wonders what future directions insect social structures would take. Some of the more recent advances could have incredible effects. For instance, ants have begun to experiment with innovations which are likely to yield more invasive effects on the ecology of the world in the future. Some plants have found ants so useful that they have started feeding them with plant foods, such as food parcels on seeds to make ants carry the seeds away. This could be regarded as a very ill-advised program for short-term gains, because it may have led ants to change to a more vegetarian diet; they have already started eating seeds, evolving special workers with nut-cracker jaws to crack them open. This has become a problem with pastoralists, because ants eat most of the seed, so that little vegetation springs up after rain for their sheep. Other ants in South and Central America have acquired a new

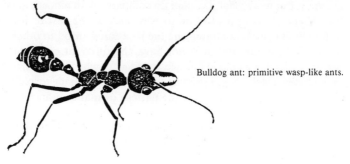

Bulldog ant: primitive wasp-like ants.

View to Eyre Bird Observatory. These inland cliffs near Cocklebiddy overlook the coastal plain which has relatively recently been raised out of the sea by earth movements across the Nullarbor. The plain is covered by coastal mallee, and the white coastal dunes in the distance are the ones threatening to cover the Bird Observatory.

Sand dunes over the Eyre Bird Observatory. These dunes were probably formed as a result of rabbit grazing and burrowing along the coast. Their activity removed roots binding the sand, and coastal winds blew it into dunes. Much work has been done to try and consolidate the dunes with vegetation, and stop them from advancing over the old telegraph station which is used as a Bird Observatory.

Major Mitchell Cockatoos. Flocks of these birds come to the Eyre Bird Observatory to drink from water provided near the house. They are an uncommon bird, sporadically seen in the arid interior of southern Australia and the North-West. (*Photo:* Graham Taylor)

Sturt pea. This plant is the floral emblem of South Australia. It grows well in depressions in the Nullarbor Plain which become wet after good rains. The large red flowers are pollinated by birds.

Pigface. This is a native species of succulent ice-plant which mainly grows around the coast and salt-lakes. The family probably originated in South Africa, and may have been carried here by birds or ocean currents many thousands of years ago. A larger, yellow/pink-flowered species has been introduced from South Africa, and is now widespread around our coasts.

Crimson chat. These brilliantly coloured birds are adapted to living in the arid interior of the country, nesting in low bushes especially near salt lakes. They feed mainly on insects.

Mallee fowl eggs. The eggs are very large for the size of the bird, and very thin shelled. This nest was dug open for research purposes, checking on the numbers of eggs and how many hatched. It was found that even the male bird tending the nest often broke the eggs by mistake.

Mallee fowl nest. Mound-building birds are found across Australia and on islands in the Pacific and Indonesian Region. Some like the brush turkey use rotting vegetation to keep the eggs warm, others, like the mallee fowl, use sand heated by the sun. Some even use volcanic heat to incubate their eggs.

technology which could take them into quite a new area of influence on the world's ecology. Instead of relying on other insects which eat plants, they have found a more direct way of using plant material. I remember seeing these parasol ants everywhere I went in Guiana, trooping off to the nest with sections of leaf. They cannot eat the leaves themselves, but use a domesticated fungus to rot the leaves and feed on the fungus instead. This ant has a profound effect on regeneration in these tropical rainforests, and if they were given a long enough evolution, could spread all over the world, diverting plant production directly into an ant-dominated ecosystem by means of its domesticated fungus. This would remove the basis of life of most other plant-eating species in the same sort of way we are affecting the world at present.

Another innovation in the social evolution of ants has been the appearance of super-societies. These occur in the ubiquitous meat-ants, which have numerous queens and form branch colonies in constant contact with one another by means of busy ant-roads. The effect is that large areas of forest or bush are controlled by a single colony — a sort of "super-society". Meat ant super-societies have already taken advantage of the food packages attached to seeds, and in the future could well evolve into a force which uses domestic animals, plants and fungi to control entire ecosystems. Other ant-traits, such as warring with neighbours and slavery, are also reminiscent of human society.

It is interesting to compare the effects of ant society with that of human society. The startling difference is that ants have had to evolve their society within the ecology of the land, because the changes have been governed by the slow rate of DNA evolution. They evolve at a similar rate to everything around them. Our society has evolved using intelligence, learning and information communicated between individuals, which effectively makes DNA technology obsolete. It is possible that human society remained in a similar condition to ants, perhaps until the Neolithic dawned. That is when people found they could consciously encourage domestic plants and animals for their own use. This change could only occur after plants and animals had had time to evolve and make use of human activities. This was a long and slow process involving adaptation to disturbance and the unconscious selection by the people for their preferred food items. The Neolithic people used these plants and animals in the same way as ants and termites do, to convert sunlight into food. However, this innovation had a profound effect on human populations, allowing them to expand and invade old ecosystems, replacing them with new ones based on the domestic animals and plants. This innovation has occurred at such a rate that the old ecosystems did not have time to adapt, while the few species that have adapted have become our pests, weeds and commensals. We are still building on this system, changing practices at an ever-increasing rate, so that there is less and less chance of species adapting and surviving which are not within our care.

It is interesting that the basic technology of the Neolithic still forms the basis of our society. The animals and plants we use are still the same ones which were used by Neolithic people: we have just pooled the species used all over the globe. Even lupins were already used by the North American Indians, and by people in the Mediterranean region, prior to their cultivation in Western Australia. What we lost through the innovation of Neolithic technology is the diverse diet enjoyed by people who have never started using domesticated species, like the Aborigines. Over a hundred plants are known to provide foodstuffs in the Rudall River Area of the Pilbara and the range of animals used may be equally diverse. This compares with many "more advanced" societies which may only cultivate one crop species and suffer severe dietary deficiencies as a consequence. It is strange that virtually no attempt is made by modern agriculturalists to diversify the number of food species used in the world, they merely "improve" the ones already in cultivation, and develop better methods of cultivation. In this respect we are still very much a modern Neolithic society.

Walking back to the track I came across a rabbit skeleton with its leg in a gin trap; the poor animal probably died a painful death, slowly dehydrating. It is remarkable how insensitive we still are about other living things, but I suppose we have little claim to be better than the ants. I remember a patoralist calmly telling me how it used to be a common practice in wild horse control, to bayonet them for the simple reason that they would disperse before they died, obviating the need to dispose of the bodies. We still have no qualms about bringing in vile diseases to kill rabbits (work is in progress on a new one, which is causing severe losses in Europe), and use gin traps without a thought, even though efficient traps are available which kill without maiming. However, all this is working in the rabbit's favour in the end, because the more rapid the process of natural selection, the more rapidly the animal adapts to the Australian environment. Pain and suffering do not affect evolution and considerable genetic differences have already been found between rabbits from different areas.

The four-wheel drive arrived and I was taken down the precipice and across the loose white sand-track to the Eyre Bird Observatory. The old building is a piece of Australian history, and one could easily imagine the little community which was in charge of this isolated telegraph station, linking Western Australia with the East. Looming over the top of the building are huge white sand dunes, powering their way inland and threatening to engulf this relic of the past. Maybe they are a monument to the stupidity of liberating rabbits into the Australian environment. It is probable that the sand became unstable when rabbits thronged along the coast in their search for food, at the time when the Nullarbor population was squeezed by the return of drought conditions. They furiously dug holes and ate sand-binding vegetation until it all blew out and heaped into mobile dunes.

More kinds of bird are seen here than in most other places in Australia.

It has the eastern species and those from the south-west. Desert species come in from the north and marine and coastal species along the shore. It even has rare Northern Hemisphere visitors such as yellow wagtails. I spent a while in a hide watching birds coming to a water trough — one of the first was a rare brush-bronzewing pigeon, then a raucous flock of Major Mitchell cockatoos arrived. I laughed to see some hanging upside down on the wires overhead, screaming at one another.

After a very pleasant stay at the Observatory my journey took me into South Australia where the surface of the Nullarbor became heavily churned by the actions of hairy-nosed wombats. It is strange that these animals have such a restricted distribution, only being found near the coast along this stretch of the Nullarbor. I stopped at one point to gaze over the cliff at the sea thundering below. One could see a dark stain in the limestone rocks where the Cretaceous gave way to the Tertiary — the last great mass extinction. How will geologists view the rocks in the future? What sort of layer will signify the present Neolithic Age?

Eventually I came to Streaky Bay in the evening, and watched the sky almost darken with a huge flock of starlings coming in to roost. They have not been allowed to become established in the West yet, but this was a frightening sight. Will they come like they did in California? They were kept out of that state for many years, using the mountain barrier, but eventually they built up into a huge population and one year an enormous flock descended from the north to colonise the area. If something like this happens in Australia, the Bird Observatory will be one of the first places to sound the warning.

Australian Raven and crows have increased greatly due to farming activity, which has provided food for adaptable scavengers. They have in recent years spread into the city suburbs in large numbers.

6 Archipelagos: Farming and Alga-Culture

The way in to Cape Arid National Park, east of Esperance, took me past regimented paddocks with tall shelterbelts of pine trees, planted in rows to reduce the rate of wind erosion. It was a veritable wildlife desert, apart from the crows which have filled the farm-scavenger niche.

At last the track began to have some native gums and banksias remaining along the edges, and I could see honeyeaters quarrelling and chasing one another across the road. The numbers of birds increased as I progressed, with flocks of spiny-cheeked honeyeaters and flights of Bourke and regent parrots. My arrival at the park was heralded by a flock of red-tailed black cockatoos. These wonderful birds seem to have an intelligent joy in flight, calling, swooping and gliding as they go over the open bushland. They have translucent patches in their tail feathers which flash bright red in the sunlight.

I drove through long stretches of heathland with a staggering variety of plants and changing vegetation. The English heaths are such a new phenomenon that only few plants have become adapted to their poor soil conditions. They were created by Neolithic and Bronze Age people only since the ice retreated 10,000 years ago, so have not had long enough to evolve such a wide variety of species. The heaths in South-West Australia have been subject to intense speciation over a period many times longer than their European counterparts, because the poor soil conditions had earlier origins and plant associations were not obliterated by tundra conditions during the ice ages. In fact weather changes during the ice ages had the opposite effect of isolating plant populations, and fostering the proliferation of new species adapted to dry heathland conditions. When Matthew Flinders circumnavigated Australia he stopped at Mt Arid in 1802, and Brown, his botanist, was fascinated by the variety of plants he found, and made an extensive collection, from which many of the known species are described.

I drove on towards Mt Arid until the track became too sandy to risk

Red-tailed black cockatoos.

continuing. I walked on, but made very slow progress, because there were so many plants to look at: creeping banksias, brown kangaroo-paws, melaleucas, one-sided bottlebrushes, lilies, silver black kingias, and many flowering mallees. Some Christmas trees were in flower, even though it was February; they tend to flower later near the cooler south coast. Some of the birds reminded me of those I had seen at the Eyre Bird Observatory, such as purple-gaped honeyeaters and purple-crowned lorikeets. In fact I was near the end of Eyre's ordeal, when he pioneered the crossing from Adelaide to Albany, which is also the route used by birds and animals crossing from east to west. Cape Arid and Israelite Bay mark the western end of the corridor, now a wildlife reserve which extends all the way to Eyre past Twilight Cove.

Coming over the brow of the hill I looked down to the southern ocean and across to islands of the Recherche Archipelago. These islands are made up of a swarm of granite hills which were deposited about 1,100 million years ago. They include Mt Arid and extend through Cape le Grand to Albany, the Porongurup Range, and to various hills near Walpole and Northcliffe.

The Islands of the Recherche are very interesting from the biological point of view because each one has a unique assemblage of species living on it. Being isolated in the ocean, few plants and animals can cross between islands or from the mainland, so each population is small and genetically distinct. These are the conditions which are ideal for generating new species over a sufficient period of time. Each population also has a high probability of dying out, because the islands are so small that natural fluctuations are likely to lead to local extinction. Because there are so many islands, over 100 in total, different assemblages of species have survived, or arrived by chance on each island, giving each its unique flora and fauna. They have also been largely spared the introduction of exotic animals and plants which have so altered the mainland. This has meant that many native species still survive which have been lost elsewhere, such as rock and tammar wallabies.

One of the startling things about the animals and plants found on the islands is that many have more affinities with those found in South Australia than those on the nearby mainland. For instance, there are eight plants common in South Australia which are only found in Western Australia on these islands, and the bandicoot living there appears to be most related to ones found on islands at the east end of the Bight. One wonders how they got there; maybe birds migrating along the coast carried the plant seeds with them, but the mammals suggest the connection may have an earlier origin. When the sea level was low during the ice ages the islands would have been part of the mainland, and during spells of wetter weather, South Australian species would have crossed along the coastal corridor. They would probably have been confined to coastal areas, because they were relatively poorly adapted to drought compared with native West Australian forms. Then as the sea advanced and drought conditions returned, they became cut-off on the islands and either died out on the mainland or had their genetic identity lost through interbreeding with local races.

I retraced my steps and rounded another headland, where I came to a sandy bay backed by a showy banksia thicket. The bird activity was incredible, with many kinds of honeyeaters and other flower seekers such as silver-eyes. Forming such pure stands, the trees have to provide food throughout the year if birds are to stay there and pollinate the flowers. So instead of having a flowering season, these trees flower all the time and support enormous numbers of birds, as well as small nectar-feeding marsupials such as the honey-possum. These banksias used to be a feature of the south coast sand plains, but most of the thickets have now been cleared for agriculture, and all the birds have gone, apart from magpies, crows and the occasional wedge-tailed eagle, which often takes on the vulture role in Australia.

On my way back through the regimented farmland, heading for Cape le Grand National Park, I began to ponder on the vectors involved in land clearance. I was driving past a huge area of farmland created by a millionaire out of coastal heathland. It is perhaps a model which illustrates the ultimate goal of modern agriculture, which seems to be centred on turning land into gold; perhaps not for the farmers alone, but for the total economy which needed the support of agricultural production during the invasive stage of European colonisation. The reliance on agricultural development made leaders ignore inconvenient warnings about the long-term consequences of exploitative land clearance and management techniques, and little thought was given to the value that uncleared land may have in the future. The general assumption has been that every piece of land should be exploited for the benefit of the economy.

The attitude was often not the fault of the farmers, who use the best advice available at the time to manage their land. It is the foundation of our society which seems to place economic development above everything else, and has no monetary value for wild animals and plants which apparently do not directly impinge on the economy. We tend to regard the future as someone else's problem, abusing the atmosphere and oceans as if they were bottomless cesspits, and clearing the last of the world's natural resources, despite the fact that most of us will see the devastating arrival of the greenhouse effect and the end of the fossil oil era. We are right in the middle of the Great Extermination, which is the root cause of the greenhouse effect, yet we seem helpless in trying to reverse the trend. It is not much use criticising countries like Brazil for removing rainforest when we have plundered and continue to plunder our natural heritage with the same sort of abandon. It all seems to emanate from a selfish Western cultural base, which regards everything as having been Created for us to use or abuse in honour of the god Mammon. We have even mortgaged the future environment by allowing the growth of debt.

We need somehow to replace this with a more ecological philosophy and set of values, recognising that we emerged within the world ecosystem and are an increasingly important part of it — the more we destroy it, the more likely we are to destroy ourselves. We have a lot to learn from some Eastern and Aboriginal cultures which regard themselves as the guardians of the countryside — the planet — instead of being its plunderers.

Passing some tall gum trees I was amazed to see a flight of purple-crowned lorikeets screaming past. They are extremely fast and energetic fliers, often going so high that one is only aware of their presence through their high-pitched screeches. Lorikeets do not rely on continuously flowering trees like the honeyeaters, as they mainly feed on gum trees which flower all at once. This means that they need to have a vagrant way of life, flying to new areas as soon as the local gums stop flowering. Each species of gum tree has a flowering season, but they flower in rather an unpredictable way, because they may not flower every year, especially during droughts or in the year following a good flowering season. Before agriculture, the lorikeets had the whole Southwest to roam over in search of flowers, but now they have to pass over long stretches of farmland. For them it is now almost as if they have to fly over a sea of desert-like agricultural land in their quest for island-like reserves of flowering gums. One wonders how many do not make it across farmland before their energy is used up, or whether they will die out when the introduced rainbow lorikeets spread out from Perth.

Lorikeets. These are rainbow lorikeets which are native to the east and north of Australia and Indonesia. A feral population became established in Perth in 1968 and is increasing in numbers. In time they may spread over much of the South-West, possibly displacing the native purple-crowned lorikeet from some of its natural range.

The lorikeets nevertheless are well adapted to persisting in an archipelago of reserves, because they have the behaviour pattern to keep recolonising them. Most other animals and nearly all plants are sedentary, like the honeyeaters, so are completely dependent on the reserve where they live. In the course of time species will fluctuate in numbers and many will die out in the same way as the faunas and floras of the Recherche Archipelago. New animals and plants will come into the reserve from time to time, but unlike islands in the past, the reserves are more like Kings Park, where most of the new species are exotic pests and weeds invading from nearby urban or agricultural land, and those becoming extinct are natives. As time goes by, one finds that the more exotics there are, the less chance natives have of survival, because of the alien agriculture-like environment the introduced species create.

In the past, when the climate fluctuated, species lived in a continuous environment, so they could follow optimal weather conditions on a continental scale over a period of time, much like the lorikeets following flowering gums. But this is not now possible, and they have to survive where they are. Weather changes brought about by the greenhouse effect will put stress on all species living in reserves and, unless we can intervene with active management, widescale extinctions are likely. Attempts are already being made to try to reduce this problem by extending road reserves and adding chains of small patches of bushland between nature reserves, to build up a matrix of corridors in the agricultural desert. It is hoped that animals and plants will be able to use these, migrating from reserve to reserve, and enhancing their chances of survival.

Coming into Cape le Grand I was greeted by bald-headed granite domes much like those of Mt Arid and the Recherche. One had caves in the top like eye-sockets in a skull. This part of the world reflects a history of Gallic exploration, when D'Entrecasteaux named many of the coastal features — Le Grand was a crew-member. It was also where Eyre had a welcome break in his ordeal when invited aboard a French whaler by Captain Rossiter.

I came to the unbelievably picturesque Lucky Bay where Matthew Flinders anchored. The sand is as near snow-white as can be, shining an almost luminous shade of blue under the breakers. Sitting overlooking the bay I watched a honey possum scurrying from flower to flower in a showy banksia. It had to dive for cover as yellow-winged honeyeaters tried to chase it off their flowers; it is extraordinary how territorial these honeyeaters are, spending an inordinate amount of energy chasing competing birds and mammals. They must gain some advantage from this behaviour, otherwise they would not do it.

Some of the birds came hopping around me expectantly, and I wondered what they were after, because honeyeaters are not attracted to the sorts of food visitors normally offer them. Then a large tabanid fly, known locally as a march fly, came to bite me. Before it had a chance, the honeyeater swooped and caught it — performing a very welcome service. However, I

Red-tailed black cockatoos. These birds are more widespread than the white-tailed species, and are found especially in the north and more arid areas, although they are also commonly seen in the karri forest. This flock was seen feeding at the roadside near the Kennedy Range east of Carnarvon.

Mt Arid. The names given to coastal features by early navigators do not always reflect the countryside. The hill has the bare granite typical of this area, but the vegetation remains green throughout the year from regular coastal rain. The flora is very rich, including the orange-leaved adenanthos in the foreground.

Recherche Archipelago. This is a swarm of granite islands east of Esperance. When sea levels were lower than at present they would have been part of the mainland, and colonised by mainland animals and plants. Since then some species have died out and others arrived, so that each island now has a unique flora and fauna. The photograph shows Mondrain Island from near Lucky Bay in Cape Le Grand National Park.

Cape Arid National Park. View to Mt Arid across Yokinup Bay. Rock parrots feed in the dunes and ground parrots still survive in low lying heathy areas.

Showy banksia thicket. This thicket behind Dolphin Cove in Cape Arid National Park is full of honeyeaters. These thickets used to be widespread in the coastal region as far as Albany, but most have been cleared for agriculture. When the land was cleared the birds would have to move elsewhere; most would die from lack of suitable habitat.

Sheep at farm dam. This is the European vision of good land management, a good stubble indicating a heavy crop, and sheep with plenty to eat during the dry summer months. For the Australian flora and fauna it is worse than the driest desert. There is no green vegetation, no photosynthesis, no shade and only unpalatable alien plants and animals to eat. This land is near Wagin—a similar picture near Esperance would show bare paddocks and blowing dust instead of the original banksia thickets.

Creeping banksia. The southern heaths contain a number of interesting plants. These banksias have a creeping underground stem so that they can avoid being killed by fires, which frequently burn through the vegetation. The flowers break through the soil, where they can be pollinated by honey possums.

Yellow winged honeyeater on showy banksia. These birds are the main pollinators of showy banksias. The trees flower throughout the year, providing a reliable food supply for the birds so that they stay there and pollinate the flowers. Other pollinators include honey possums, which are often chased off the flowers by these quarrelsome birds.

Lucky Bay, Cape Le Grand. Matthew Flinders stopped here on his way around Australia. The beach is made up of a very pure silica sand. The vegetation on the granite hills has many interesting plants, including a thick-leaved hakea and a red clawflower *(Calothamnus)*.

Ornate cowfish. The water in the bays is usually very clear and full of fish including sea dragons (a kind of seahorse) and porcupine fish. The cowfish is heavily armoured so does not need to flee from predators. It is colourful and slow swimming.

Honey-possum. Ranges from Eneabba to Eyre mainly living in heathland areas where there are banksias and myrtles flowering all year.

Yellow-winged honeyeater eating a march-fly. Honeyeaters catch many insects to provide protein in their diet; they have learnt to catch marchflies attacking visitors to Cape Le Grand National Park.

soon found that the flies arrived at a greater rate than the birds could catch them, and the honeyeaters started taking the ones I killed in preference to catching their own! After that the kangaroos came begging for bread, and fairly sizzled with march flies.

When I had first visited this national park fourteen years earlier there were no tame animals like this. It is amazing how in time they become fearless of people. The same process has run for much longer in other parts of Australia, where possums flock around campers at night and kangaroos are beginning to become a menace, reminiscent of bears in American parks. This is all part of the process which leads to domestication, and to adaptations which are suitable for animals and plants to survive in European agricultural and urban landscapes. In the European environment most species either became extinct long ago or changed to exploit unnatural environments. In fact many rare and endangered species in Britain today are not the original inhabitants of wildwood Britain, but those which became successful exploiters of the severely altered landscape created by people since the Neolithic. Many had evolved to use land which was farmed on a rotational basis, used for sheep grazing, and for coppiced woodland (cut for fencing, poles and firewood every five years or so). The revolution in land use this century, together with operations of the Forestry Commission, have so changed traditional forms of land management that the species adapted to these conditions have no suitable habitat left. They include the corncockle, pasqueflower and harvest mouse.

In a welcome move, some of this attractive flora is now being re-created along motorways and other roadsides in England, and seed production for such projects has become a profitable business. Similar work is progressing in parts of Australia, where new roadworks are being seeded with native plants both to make the roadside more attractive and to reduce erosion problems.

I looked out over the bay and saw silver gulls quarrelling noisily, and then several Pacific gulls came over. This gull is huge in comparison, and makes calls which are reminiscent of European gulls — like the background gull-calls one often hears during seaside scenes in Australian films and radio-plays! Then I saw a huge white-breasted sea-eagle wheeling overhead, making its way towards the granite hills. I walked to the top of the nearest hill, only to see the eagle disappear around the next headland. I sat down and while looking into the dark water of Lucky Bay I saw a large sunfish lazily flopping around near the surface, with its tall fin coming out of the water from time to time. I had often wondered why these fish have such an odd shape, almost circular and flat with two long fins projecting up and down from near where the tail ought to be. They can grow to an enormous size, almost two metres in diameter. It appeared to be feeding, and using binoculars I could see it was eating jellyfish. Not many animals eat jellyfish, but it is interesting that the sunfish has a similar profile to some of the marine turtles which also subsist on this diet. I could see that the jellyfish were at the surface, and the fish tended to swim on its side, drifting under the waves to catch them. These fish must be fairly frequent visitors to this part of the coast, because I usually see some each time I go there.

I later went snorkelling in the cold southern water, and found that some of the jellyfish were a kind of stinging, box jellyfish. It is a small species, well known to swimmers in the Southwest as Busselton stingers, or erroneously as bluebottles. (Bluebottles are a floating species related to the Portuguese man-o'war jellyfish, which gets blown on shore during winter; they are easy to see and get blamed for the stings caused in summer by the box jellyfish, which is invisibly transparent.) The sea was full of life common along southern shores, such as large seaweeds, porcupine fish, cowfish, flotillas of cuttlefish and huge abalones stuck on the rocks deep under the water. Few of the larger fish remain through the pressure of fishing, and I saw none of the large rays which were common, gliding and basking in the shallows, fifteen years ago.

Driving on towards Esperance the road took me through long stretches of low-lying dune-slack country with swamps and rush-filled pasture. I wondered how this country would fare as the greenhouse effect takes hold. The climatic effect may not be great because the land is so near the coast, but as the sea warms, the sea level may rise a metre or so in the next fifty years, which will turn good agricultural land into coastal swamp. Could this mean that all the birdlife associated with these areas, which have been so depleted by draining and filling in the last 100 years, could return? According to recent evidence, change could occur very suddenly, perhaps within as little as ten years in response to changes in greenhouse gases. It appears that the gases may build up to a critical level, then the weather systems controlling climate become unstable and change to a new regime, as already occurs with the El Nino phonomenon. Another suggestion is that the Western Antarctic ice sheet could suddenly break up, speeding climatic change and a sea level rise of five metres. Farmers will have to live with the possibility that one day a drought may come which will not end, and will signify that the climate has flipped. The effects on farming will be as devastating as those on wildlife, cut off in island-like reserves.

Climatologists have built up models which predict climatic changes and have used them to map areas of the globe which they think most likely to benefit from climate change and those which will be disadvantaged. It is hard to appreciate what they represent in terms of human suffering and loss of natural ecosystem. Huge areas of land will no longer be suitable for agriculture, while other areas which supported residual natural ecosystems will be progressively invaded by agriculture. These in themselves will have global impacts, but there will also be an increase in the number of natural disasters caused by unprecedented weather extremes as the climate changes. Is there an answer, or do we just wait for the inevitable?

Impending doom has been a preoccupation of most societies, especially those based on Christianity. Every age has brought people who prophesy doom; the day when we pay for our sins. With the coming of Malthus and mathematics, scientists have long known that there is an end point to the growth in human populations. The fact that our activity is now having repercussions in terms of global climatic change means that the day is getting close.

What has brought us to this condition? I wonder whether it is not so much the global human population that is the problem, but how we use the planet. It all seems to have started when animals and plants became adapted to living near human populations and the Neolithic people learned how to exploit them as domesticated species. Our society is the natural extension of this phase, which is still dependent upon these same animals and plants. We have now just about reached the global population limit that can be supported by this technology, especially as we continue hunter-gatherer activities of netting ocean fish and felling rainforests. We effectively are continuing to live in the Neolithic phase, even though we are driving tractors, using artificial fertilisers and applying genetic engineering, because we have still not found an alternative to using species domesticated in prehistoric times.

Just past Esperance I turned in to look at Pink Lake, a curious salt lake with a pink coloured water and white salt embankments. To me this lake signifies what could be the turning point; the beginning of the Post-Neolithic Age, the factor which could postpone Armageddon, reverse the greenhouse effect, save the forests and allow the human race to continue as a species. It shows to me an alternative technology which could replace the Neolithic reliance on a relatively inefficient use of animals and plants to produce food and materials from the sun's energy.

At Pink Lake a program began which harnessed natural algae as domestic species to produce materials for foodstuffs. It is one of many such ventures around the world harnessing algae and microbes known as cyanobacteria (they used to be known as blue-green algae). These microbes formed one of the main stepping stones in the origin of animals and plants on Earth, and were responsible for producing our atmosphere of oxygen by pioneering the process of photosynthesis. Given an aquatic environment and sources of carbon dioxide and necessary minerals, they can produce organic matter at an incredible rate compared with our domestic plants and animals. The pioneering work here has led to the use of algae to manufacture food additives, in the form of carotenoids. The production has extended to the Hutt Inlet north of Geraldton, where the production rate is faster due to the higher temperatures and largely uninterrupted sunlight. Cyanobacteria and alga-culture has long been advocated as a means of providing food for the Third World, and considerable advances have been made over the years. It is interesting that the early work centred on making protein from crude oil, because it did not seem to occur to many people that it could be disastrous to make huge populations reliant on a limited, non-renewable resource. I believe the new approach should be for this technology to provide food and materials for the developed world on a sustainable basis.

Huge food technology companies are already able to produce hamburgers and bread from base materials far removed from beef and wheat. My vision is of them undertaking the research necessary to create staple food items such as these from algal base materials, processing them with genetically engineered bacteria and fungi. This would create the new farming technology, where the base material would be produced at rates that "late Neolithic" farmers would find unbelievable. For instance, cyanobacteria grown commercially in ponds elsewhere to make food products can produce at up to about fifty times the rate of wheat (between 20 and 55 tonnes/ha dry weight compared with 1 or 2 tonnes/ha for wheat.) A by-product of this new activity would be that it would create a high demand for waste products such as carbon dioxide, sulphates, nitrates and phosphates, which are now pumped into the ocean and atmosphere. Other advantages are that it could produce year round, use salt water, work best in arid areas, and be largely independent of the vagaries of climate. The industry could also be combined with solar power generators, fresh-water distillation and gas-production plants making methane or hydrogen.

Food production need only be the first step of the new age. Bacteria are already being used to produce bacterial cellulose to make special papers, and bacterial plastics have also been made. If this went on-line in general production, felling trees for paper would pass into history, maybe even for timber, reserving wood for expensive furniture and veneers. Trees may even come to be regarded as most valuable when they are standing, alive in the forest. I do not see this technology replacing most of our current farming activities, but mainly fulfilling bulk requirements of our society. Fruit and vegetables would still be in great demand, but I hope most animal products would be replaced by such things as beef and chicken proteins produced by genetically engineered bacteria.

One can only guess at what the new "farms" would look like. They are unlikely to be open ponds, except where bacterial pellets are being fed to prawns and fish. Maybe the land will be covered by transparent channels made out of bacterial plastics, bright green in colour from burgeoning algae, all leading to refinery-like buildings where the material is bio-engineered by bacteria and fungi into an array of secondary products. The cost of such developments may make them appear totally unrealistic to modern industrialists and politicians. But the spectre of a gap appearing between demand and supply in world wheat production and the drying up of fossil fuel resources, let alone the necessity to reverse the greenhouse effect, may lead to direct financial incentives to develop this new technology. One can almost hear the cry for "alga-power" to save our future.

This technology has so much potential value resting on it that its research and development costs are likely to seem as unimportant in the future, as those which brought million-dollar computers of a few years ago onto everyone's desk, and quartz chronometers down to the three-dollar model I now wear. It is amusing to think that this advance into harnessing microbes to trap the energy from the sun and converting it into food, energy and material production, would be equivalent to that made by parasol ants and termites when they evolved the ability to grow domestic fungi on artificial compost heaps. Soon we will have plundered the globe's stored resources and fossil energy, its soil, forests and minerals to such an extent that we will have to turn to alternatives in order to survive. If we are unable to make the change, the lemmings have demonstrated what will happen; the world population will be drastically cut by mechanisms outside our control, maybe leading to the extinction of the human race. The ants are already a step ahead of us; can we learn from them, or are we doomed to let them take our place?

Tammar Wallaby. Once extended from near Perth to South Australia, now restricted to a few localities, and to off-shore islands such as Garden Island, an island in the Recherche Archipelago and Kangaroo Island in South Australia.

Potoroo *(Potorous platyops)*. Reconstructed from Gould's Drawings and a living relative. This species used to occur in the south-west but is now presumed extinct: it is thought to have been on the verge of extinction prior to European settlement.

7 The Fitzgerald River: Changing Climates and New Landscapes

I always experience an incredible feeling of expectancy when entering the Fitzgerald River National Park. It is akin to entering a lost world where relics of past ages persist in isolation. When approaching from Hopetoun one is struck by curious banksias with upside-down flowers, and the strangely geometric forms of the Barrens regelia bottlebrush. Further on there are groves of the royal hakea; an extraordinary plant which at first looks more like one of the succulent plants growing on Mt Kilimanjaro, or even a cactus. A closer look at the plants on the slopes reveals that most are unique species, only found growing in parts of the park. One has a feeling that one may stumble across similar animal relics, like potoroos or a noisy scrub-bird, though neither has been found yet. However, the dibbler, a small marsupial once thought to be extinct, has been found surviving near the northern boundary of the park, and several rare birds are still living there, such as the bristlebird, western whipbird and ground parrot.

I climbed East Mt Barren to take in the view over unlimited bushland as far as the eye can see, the park extending over a magnificent 243,000 hectares as far as Bremer Bay fifty kilometres away. I was reminded of my first visit in 1970 when I joined a group of like-minded people in a desperate bid to save the area from alienation. It was in the middle of the Poseidon mining boom time, when there was a casino-like atmosphere. Every mineral show, whether legitimate or not, was being turned into a South-Sea Bubble by entrepreneurs who were in a position to prey on a world of cashed-up investors. We had come to provide scientific data on which to base a case against granting mining rights, to be fought three weeks hence in the Mining Warden's Court. It was an extraordinary situation, because this was still a frontier state, which was desperate for economic growth at any cost. Land development was an unquestioned goal, and legislation did not cover such matters as conservation interests in regard to mineral exploitation. The only venue for such cases was quite inappropriately the Mining Warden's Court, which was designed for dealing with disputed claims, and was not geared to hearing about flora, fauna, conservation, and preservation of natural scenery in national parks.

When we arrived at the Fitzgerald River, we found feverish activity, with pegging parties driving a mosaic of tracks through the bush, setting aside whole mountains for aggregate quarries to supply the building construction industry, vast river flats for open-cast coalmining, and a range of other mines and quarries extending from stonemasonry to heavy metal ores. Some had even been drilling for oil. The area had not been under such a serious threat before, so little data existed on the wildlife present. We did the best we could under the circumstances, because it was not a good time for biological surveys; it was in the middle of winter, with cold frosty mornings, and there had been a long drought which had caused animal populations to decline. A vast fire had also been started near the Gairdner River, which had burnt through much of the Park fifteen months previously, temporarily destroying the habitat. We hoped to find potoroos in the middle of the proposed coalmining area, to catch the public imagination and give conservation a political edge. Mostly we only found rabbits, foxes and house mice, because the pegged areas were still recovering from disturbance caused during previous mining and exploration activity, and exotic weeds were spreading as a result of the fire. However the relatively pristine nature of the rest of the park and its unique flora made its potential value as a conservation area immediately obvious, while its scenery ranked it high as a potential national park. The public outcry in the press and activities behind the scenes led to the case being withdrawn from the Court the day I was due to appear, and moves were set in motion for the area to be set aside as a national park. These moves were later aided by the bursting of the Poseidon bubble, which took the pressure out of the mining-boom fever for a decade and allowed time for the public to evolve a greater environmental consciousness.

The park was still not safe, and further battles were fought with the farming lobby to prevent more land on the northern boundary from being released for agriculture. The frontier attitude towards land release was clearly demonstrated by the politicians of the time boasting about clearing a million acres a year. The attitude was so ingrained that even the Department of Agriculture was prepared to release land for farming in some areas which were known to be extremely marginal. This battle was only won in 1983 when many people, including the farmers, were pointing out the problems of salinity, soil degradation, erosion, drought and debt in relatively good farming land, let alone marginal areas like the Fitzgerald River.

Pressure for mining and exploration continue, and are likely to surface from time to time in tune with the stock market. One must expect pressure groups to use such ploys as: "Mining in national parks should be regarded as a legitimate use of the area, causing minimal disturbance", or that "This potential source of revenue should not be locked away in the ground for ever, because the Australian economy needs to be propped up by mining activity". One is led to question motives when it is clear that mining is a once-off operation and must decline in importance. Most seem to forget that the economy is a living thing, evolving with the times. In the past it has moved from being farm-based to mineral-based, and is now dominated by the service industries. Tourism has an unbelievable potential, now that people from all over the world are seeking places which have not been subject to recent human exploitation. To these tourists, locating a mine in a national park is rather like placing a casino in the aisle of a cathedral.

William the Conqueror probably had little inkling of what he was creating for future generations when he imposed Forest Law on the area which became the New Forest in England. We similarly may not have much idea what the future holds for our national parks; at present they are holding grounds for natural scenery, native wildlife and plants — and minerals. If the minerals are not mined they are not squandered, and like the animals and plants, they will be kept for future generations. They will still be there in the distant future, and could be mined if the need for minerals becomes greater than other values found in the area. On the other hand, if they are mined now, the minerals will soon be gone for ever, taking much of the aesthetic and conservation value of the mineralised area with them. It is also the time when Australian ecosystems are under greatest stress from clearance and introduced plants and animals; what is left needs to be preserved to allow time for at least some species to adapt to our alien managed landscapes.

It is interesting to compare our national parks with those in England. Australia's are quite different, because they are remnants of the original countryside, containing incredible resources of natural ecosystem. The English parks are scenic areas of environment long subject to severe human disturbance, and were created just as if a scenic part of the wheat-belt, including towns and active mines, were declared a national park. The English national parks are very attractive in themselves, but if some had the wealth of pristine vegetation enjoyed by our parks and were made up of the original British "wildwood", they would surely be vigorously protected from disturbance. However, their vegetation is instead dependent upon long established human disturbance, so the management of the English parks requires an entirely different approach, involving the continuance of farming, grazing, forestry, etc.

Near the top of East Mt Barren there were groves of a mallee with large yellow flowers. It is similar to the more widely distributed bell-fruited mallee *Eucalyptus preissiana*, but has been isolated long enough on the hills in the Fitzgerald River to have evolved into a distinct species known as *Eucalyptus coronata*. It made a beautiful picture with the red-flowered Barrens regelia, white rocks and blue sea.

The mountains in the park form part of the system which threw up the Stirling Range. The rocks were originally laid down in a shallow sea prior to about 1,300 million years ago, with those in East Mt Barren mainly being

Royal hakea. This unusual shrub only grows in the Fitzgerald River National Park. There is a particularly good stand of it on the slopes of East Mt Barren. It is growing here with some showy banksia.

East Mt Barren. A rockface near the top showing the white quartzite of the mountain. This rock originated as a silica sand and was crushed into rock during the mountain-building process. The plants include the red-flowered barrens regelia, which only grows on some of the hilltops in the Fitzgerald River National Park.

Mid Mt Barren. The survey done in 1970 suggested that the Fitzgerald River Class 'C' Reserve merited it being made into a National Park.

Spongelite cliffs. View from the side of the Fitzgerald River gorge to Mid Mt Barren. The cliffs are made up of silica sponge spicules from the skeletons of sponges. These sponges inhabited the sea when it was higher and the mountains were off-shore islands.

Red lechenaultia. This species seems to do best in disturbed soils on firebreaks and tracks. Another, taller species, is restricted to the tops of a few of the mountains.

Scarlet banksia. This attractive species only occurs near the south coast between Albany and Hopetoun.

a quartz sand. Then, when the granite of the Porongurups to the Recherche Archipelago were forced in, the flat sandstones were squeezed, heated and bent to form a hard white quartzite. Over the millions of years since, the land surface has been worn away, leaving the harder rocks standing up as mountains. The edge of the range was squeezed particularly hard, producing a finely layered rock, shining with mica and garnet crystals. These hard crystals form a dark coarse sand along the rocky shores.

Looking down to the base of the mountain, I could see that it spreads out in a skirt before falling away in cliffs to the sea. This shows how much the land has risen in the last few million years, with the level area representing the old shore line. The land movement which lowered and raised the coast was the same one which inundated the Nullarbor. This makes the view west to Mid Mt Barren even more interesting, because about 48 million years ago the land would have been full of coastal reed-filled swamps responsible for depositing the brown coals. After this the land sank further and allowed the sea to flow far inland so that an observer would be sitting on an offshore island, looking over a turbulent southern ocean, battered by the roaring forties, to other distant islands made up of the Whoogurup Range, Mid Mt Barren, Annie Peak and so on.

The seabed at the time was covered in sponges which used silica in the water to build their skeletons. These silica spicules were deposited over the ocean floor, forming a thick layer of spongelite rock characteristic of the Fitzgerald River. During the next 16 million years when the ranges were offshore islands, the flora evolved in isolation and set in motion the evolution of the unique flora of the area. Then the land rose out of the water again, uniting all the islands with the mainland. However, the spongelite deposited between the hills altered the soil composition in such a way that the flora could not spread and was still largely isolated. This allowed the evolution to continue, yielding such strange species as the royal hakea.

The Fitzgerald River itself cuts through the soft spongelite siltstone producing a wide gorge with picturesque cream or yellow coloured cliffs, sculptured by wind and rain. Some parts of the cliff have been cut off from the gorge and jut starkly out of the river valley, like the flat-topped Roe's Rock, named after the Surveyor-General, Septimus Roe. During my July visit after the drought, the river was merely a chain of salt-encrusted pools, with water only flowing through the sand. But strand lines showed that huge volumes of water flow down the river in times of flood, with as much as one-sixth of the volume of the Ord River in flood (W.A.'s largest river). All these factors emphasise the problems farmers have to face when trying to manage their land in the Fitzgerald River catchment, and lend weight to the argument that no more land should be released in this area. The river had already become salted from land clearance and had lost most of its original fauna, while the area was clearly prone to long drought periods and sudden deluges. The soil derived from the siltstone was fine-grained and lacked anything to bind it, making it subject to severe erosion problems. I remember reading about roads in the area being blocked by drifts of topsoil blown off the paddocks.

Viewing some of these problems led me to suggest research projects based on the ecology of abandoned farmland. This seemed an interesting line to follow, since this was a legitimate line of study in America, where "oldfields" were an important feature of the countryside. I had even studied squirrels in a national park based on abandoned farmland in North Carolina and had been in charge of nature reserves in Britain based on abandoned farmland. However, this line of research proved to be somewhat premature; I can distinctly remember the incredulity expressed by some agricultural scientists at the time, who had never seen this as an end-point for new farms. Their entire careers had been built on the methods of bringing new areas of bushland into agricultural production.

Things are different now, millions of dollars are being spent on research, fencing and trying to revegetate farmland which has had to be taken out of production through salt encroachment. It is only a matter of time before the other forms of degradation have to be addressed, because it is increasingly being realised that farming for export is very like mining minerals for export: instead of minerals being lost to the country for ever, it is Australia's soils which are being lost. One calculation suggests that five tonnes of soil are lost for every tonne of wheat produced.

The Fitzgerald River is probably going to be one of the most important centres in Australia for this form of research, because the local farming community is only too aware of the problems caused by land clearance. In 1983, for example, they experienced the problems of wind erosion, waterlogging and erosion, salinity, decline of native vegetation, rising water tables, non-wetting sands, soil structure decline, and pasture deterioration. In that year they clubbed together with their one-time opposition — conservation lobbyists — and are engaged in an active project to protect the region, which covers the whole Fitzgerald River catchment area. This followed the selection of the Fitzgerald River in 1978 as an international biosphere reserve under the UNESCO Man and the Biosphere program. This was intended to provide a network of reserves covering all the main world ecosystems, so that genetic diversity was preserved and environmental

Blue-tongue *(Tiliqua occidentalis)*.

change could be monitored. The Fitzgerald Biosphere Project aims to promote conservation with development in the region.

Since my first visit I can now see that the salted areas are fast becoming some of the future "oldfields", and was reminded of a wonderful wetland I visited in 1968 near Purdue in Indiana. It was once agricultural land, but had been turned into a game reserve where pheasants were reared for sport. The secondary woodland and swamp had become an important wildlife refuge and had been singled out as a resting place by migrating sandhills cranes. I was privileged to see the flock of about 2,000 birds, representing most of the world's remaining population of the species, wheel up into the sky and parade past my viewpoint.

Salted wetlands here will almost certainly become important wildlife refuges, and maybe even become nature reserves and national parks in the future. Some salt lakes, such as Lake Dumbleyung, are already wildfowl reserves and support enormous populations of ducks and swans. At the moment Australia is being scoured for suitable native plants and trees to revegetate salted land, and the country is being dotted with trial plantings. In the future we will see similar activity with regard to land subject to insufferable drought conditions, wind erosion, compaction and so on. That is when the floras of biosphere reserves and national parks will become the invaluable sources of the new vegetations.

In the meantime many farmers have the unenviable task of keeping going on land which probably should never have been cleared, and certainly not have been subject to modern farming techniques. This is perhaps where the greatest progress in farming can be made, because modern farming methods are the main cause of the loss of the land. The same problems are appearing in Europe. Traditional farming techniques evolved in Britain allowed farmland to be cultivated for thousands of years, and still be productive. These included rotations, leaving the land fallow, and conserving humus by using manure and ploughing in vegetation. It also involved selective use of the land, with low-lying areas used as meadows, steep uplands and poorer soils as woods, and all having hedges and shelterbelts to protect the land from wind and water erosion. This form of land management preserved the soil structure and soil fauna and flora. But modern farming tends to use heavy, soil-compacting machinery, adds chemical fertilisers, uses herbicides, prevents the accumulation of organic matter by killing weeds and burning stubble, and regularly disturbs the soil and crops annually. The land is also totally cleared, hill and valley, with furrows often running up and down hills, causing gullies which choke rivers with silt, and expose it all to wind erosion. The humus is quickly dissipated as carbon dioxide gas, the soil fauna and flora die from exposure and lack of food, water retention and wetting abilities are lost, and a healthy soil structure is destroyed, causing erosion, compaction and salting problems. It is interesting how the onset of this process was well-known to farmers who dug dams in newly cleared land to provide water for their stock. The dams would remain empty for two or three years until the soil fauna died, especially the ants and termites, then the pores in the soil collapsed, the rain water no longer soaked in and the dams began to fill.

Charles Darwin's observation that the health of earthworms can be equated with the health of the soil has been strongly endorsed regarding the general soil fauna. Now eminent soil scientists are advocating, in the strongest terms, a return to more traditional farming methods as a way of rescuing the soil, and to set the industry on a course which can be sustained indefinitely into the future. This would mean, amongst other things, that whole regions need to be re-examined in relation to topography, drainage and soil type, and new maps drawn out delineating paddocks for rotations, salt meadow areas, protected swamplands, and areas of poor soils open for the regrowth of scrub or heath. Farm boundaries may also need redefining and the whole would be dependent upon the cooperation of local communities. This is perhaps where the Fitzgerald Biosphere Project may be heading. If there are any local Aborigines left who can remember some of the traditional ways, they may also be able to provide invaluable data to help plan this reconstruction process.

It is curious how one can miss the obvious reasons for some commonplace observations. It was while coming down East Mt Barren that one of these finally struck me. It involved skidding down some quartzite screes which brought back childhood memories of mountain-climbing in the English Lake District. As is often the case, the memories were conjured up by a smell; one that is familiar to anyone who hits rock against rock. I suddenly pieced this together with an experience of going down a scree of flintstones at night in Dorset, when my feet became surrounded by a constellation of sparks. It was obvious: the sparks ionise the oxygen in air and form ozone gas, which has this characteristic smell. (This gas is a very reactive form of oxygen which has molecules made up of three atoms instead of the normal two.)

I could not help my mind drifting into the role of ozone in the upper atmosphere and the ozone "hole" which has been extending over this area of southern Australia in the month of December. What effect is this going to have on the Biosphere Project? Ozone depletion is caused by gases such as CFCs and volcanic chlorine reaching the upper atmosphere, and reacting with ozone in the presence of sunlight. The effects of ozone reduction are that its screening action on sunlight is lost, and we can expect more ultraviolet light reaching the ground. One of the main uses we have for this light at the moment is in sterilising articles, because it kills bacteria, as well as its commonly known action of damaging the skin. Ozone depletion not only increases the amount of the sun's energy reaching the ground, it inhibits plant growth, particularly algae in the southern ocean. This compounds the greenhouse effect, because oceanic algae are one of the main lungs of the world in removing the prime cause of the greenhouse effect: the increasing levels of carbon dioxide in the atmosphere. The most likely climatic effects in Southwest Australia are thought to be an increasing level of aridity, with a marked increase in the frequency and severity of droughts. The already marginal nature of farmland in the area underlines the urgency for action to prevent the formation of a dustbowl and the choking of the Fitzgerald River National Park with silt and sand.

When I came down to the road it was sad to see some dead banksias which had been killed by jarrah dieback disease. Jarrah is fairly resistant to the fungus, but the banksias, dryandras and other proteaceous plants are severely affected. It is a soil-borne fungus largely spread by earth-moving equipment and on vehicle tyres and bodywork, so roads and off-road exploration vehicles have brought the fungus into the park. Urgent action is being taken to try to inhibit further spread, with all vehicles entering the park being sterilised, and eventually it is hoped that all the roads will be sealed and drained.

The road took me past a wonderful grove of royal hakea, and I noticed that a large one had a bundle of dead grasses stuffed between its branches, which proved to be a red-eared fire-tailed finch's nest. This was a surprise find during my first visit in 1970, because this species is mainly found in the wet south-west corner of the state. At that time this was the most easterly record for the species, but since then my sons have found them nesting at Cape le Grand, and they are also present at Cape Arid. The road went over a hill, where a spindly willow-like tree gracefully hung its trailing branches overhead. The flowers and nuts were unmistakably those of a eucalypt, even though it did not look anything like a gum tree. It proved to be the weeping gum *Eucalyptus sepulcralis*: yet another species restricted to the park. Along the roadsides were many melaleucas in flower and a unique plant, *Daviesia pachyphylla* belonging to the pea family, which has succulent thorns. Another interesting plant is related to the banjines but does not look like one at all. This is the qualup bell (*Pimelia physodes*), which has evolved a flower structure which looks almost identical to quite a different family — the mountain bells (*Darwinia*) found in the Stirling Range. It must use similar pollinators to these flowers for the flower structures to have converged in this way. I went to look at the plants and a shiny blue-tongue skink hissed at me from the shade of a melaleuca.

I reluctantly left the park and headed west. As I drove along I was pleased to see evidence that the farming community was doing something about land-degradation problems. Salted areas were being fenced off, and young trees were beginning to dot the landscape. Many had cut contour ditches on slopes to reduce soil erosion, and planted shelterbelts of local trees. All this would have been unthinkable in the 1970s when the bulldozers were the most active form of land management, clearing millions of hectares of arid bushland.

I turned south from the main highway along some dirt roads past Mt Manypeaks and headed for Two Peoples Bay. This had been destined for a new township in the early '60s, but after it had been surveyed in 1961 a bird was heard in the thick vegetation covering the new town site. It was the long-lost noisy scrub-bird. It had been widespread during the early days of settlement, living in dense scrub and sedges surrounding swamps adjoining jarrah/marri forest between Waroona and Albany. It was rarely seen, but the males are territorial and can readily be heard by their characteristic calls. Its loss was caused by the breakdown of Aboriginal society and their traditional land management, and its replacement by European management, which involved frequent burning, drainage and grazing of swamps. This rapidly removed all the bird's habitat, and the last one was thought to have died in 1889. It appears that this isolated population survived at Two Peoples Bay because Mt Gardner acts as a shield against firefronts entering during summer, and when fire did come, it only burned part of the area because the mountain's bare rock faces acted as firebreaks.

After the area had been reclassified as a reserve, it was managed to try and prevent uncontrolled fires, and the bird population has increased from about 40 singing males in 1962, to 200 in 1987. The program has been so successful that birds have been taken to the Mt Manypeaks Reserve and a new population has been established there, and further introductions are taking place elsewhere. This program reminds me of the sandhills crane in America which declined to a population of about 200, but with conservation measures has now increased to more than 3,000 birds. Maybe the day will come when some of the abandoned salted land to the north will develop thick enough scrub and forest for noisy scrub-birds to recolonise there.

It is fascinating how the presence of one rare species is so often the indicator of others. While walking around the reserve I noticed many large dark butterflies flipping away, flashing dark purple hues. They turned out to be the rare large brown azure (*Ogyris idmo idmo*). Little is known about the butterfly, but azure butterflies have close associations with ants as larvae, being protected by them and often taken into their nests over inclement seasons. The large blue butterfly in England had a similar association, and it lived in areas with a short calcareous turf created by sheep grazing, but it is now extinct because of the loss of sheep grazing and the decline of chalk-pastures.

The large brown azure probably also needs a complex association of factors for survival, which include a dependence on conditions being right for its ants, as well as its food plant. Management for the birds may be preserving a number of other species such as this butterfly, which are dependent upon pockets of land managed in order to retain pre-European conditions. This may tide the species over the period of maximum habitat destruction now in operation, and allow recolonisation as previously cleared land reverts to patches of secondary bushland in the future.

Chittick *(Lambertia inermis)*, an orange-flowered shrub which flowers all year in heathy areas from the Stirling Range to Cape Arid.

8 The Stirlings: Atmosphere and Climate

I always find it a bit tantalising driving to the Stirling Range. One glimpses the jagged outline of the range from the top of a rise, then plunges into undulating paddocks. After many kilometres one comes to another viewpoint to look over the countryside, but the range appears to be little closer than it was before. This may go on for an hour, with the hills only slowly becoming closer, because the atmosphere is usually so clear that one can see the range when it is over a hundred kilometres away. The roadsides and paddocks have remnants of the original forest gum trees, especially the flat-topped yates in the valleys which have erect branches spreading from near the base in the form of a cone. Claypan areas often have groves of moort gums, which are dense little bushes with dark rounded leaves, quite unlike any other gum tree.

Coming from Gnowangerup in the early morning, the land dipped down towards the range and was filled with a sea of mist in which the hilltops floated like a chain of islands. Dew sparkled in the green paddocks, especially around the shadow of the observer, so that it formed a glowing halo. Then the road dipped down into the cold billowing fog where the roadsides became festooned with the skeletal remains of upturned rootstocks and fractured branches. A severe windstorm had been through the area a few months earlier, sweeping across the bare paddocks and toppling the remaining yate trees.

The road began to rise again and came out of the fog near Mt Trio, where tongues of dispersing mist crept up its slopes and billowed over the top. I turned off the road along the corrugated gravel track to Toolbrunup Peak. Groves of pink-flowered scallops hakea sprouted from the graded trackside like a weed. This is one of the few native species which respond well to soil disturbance, and readily colonise roadworks. Its leaves are reminiscent of royal hakea, and the two species probably had a common ancestor millions of years ago. Most of the other vegetation was similar to that of the dry southern heaths I had seen stretching from Cape Arid to the Fitzgerald River.

Further up the track there were straggly chittick bushes with geometrically arranged orange flowers. They seem to flower all year round, using the strategy of continuously producing a few seeds, so that at least some escape being found by seed-eating insects. Other plants use the alternative strategy of flowering in profusion over a short period, so that insects are swamped by food and do not have long enough to breed into large populations and eat all the seeds. But nothing is as simple as that. The Stirling Range bottlebrush also seems to flower all year, possibly adopting this strategy in order to provide a consistent food source for its pollinators. It also retains its seeds in the living seedheads for years until they are released by a fire, so theoretically the insect populations could breed up to eat them all. However, the woody nut appears to protect the seeds from most insects as well as from being burned by fire. Other factors may also be in operation, as with the banksias mentioned in Chapter 3. These also flower all year and hold their seeds in woody cones, but are dependent upon black cockatoos controlling the seed-eating insects which burrow through the cones.

The footpath leading up the mountain soon took me into a deep, shady, scree-bordered gully full of marri trees, and I could hear the sound of running water amplified by the rocky border of the creek below. These conditions can only be created by mountains in such dry country, and produce habitats which may be suitable for animals and plants a long way from their normal range, such as those normally living in the wet southwest corner of the state. I came across some oak-leaved *Chorileana* and karri hazel and then noticed some large leaves, like those of a gum tree, growing out of the ground. After searching for a while I found one with a tall spike topped by the remains of a brownish flower — it was a slipper orchid. These only grow in very moist shady conditions, and have probably been isolated here for a long time.

Slipper orchids are an attractive group of orchids, which includes many of the world's rarest and most sought-after species. They are thought to represent the stock from which other orchids evolved, and retain primitive features. This is one of only two species known in Australia, and flowers during the summer from November usually until as late as April. But this one had only just finished flowering in June. I was reminded of the elbow orchid I had seen on the Darling Scarp, which duped a male thynnid wasp into pollinating it. The slipper orchid has turned its attention to an ichneumon wasp instead. The whole flower mimics a female wasp and the males are attracted by the female-like scent emitted by the flower. Duped by the flower's anatomy, the male inserts his body into the cavity of the flower, trying to mate with it, but when he withdraws his body, one can

Stirlings bottlebrush and Bluff Knoll. One of the many plants endemic to the range.

Kangaroo with Toolbrunup Peak behind. Visitors to Bluff Knoll in the Stirling Range National Park now have kangaroos hopping up to them and demanding to be fed.

Helmet orchid. This unusual orchid grows in deep shade in damp places under rocks and in ravines. Its deep red flowers only come out in mid winter. It is probably pollinated by fungus gnats.

View from the top of Toolbrunup Peak. Mt Hassell is in the foreground with Bluff Knoll and other eastern peaks in the distance.

Mt Trio. An evening view from Mt Hassell. The rocks in the foreground show fossil ripple marks dating from when the rock was laid down as sand in a shallow sea, perhaps 1,700 million years ago.

Mountain bell *(Darwinia leiostyla)*. Several species of these striking flowers are found only in the Stirling Range National Park. Each species is confined to a few mountain tops, and probably date from the time when the hills formed a chain of off-shore islands, isolated from one another. Or it may have been ice age droughts which isolated them on the hilltops.

Porongurup Range. This range is built of the granite which stretches as far as the Recherche Archipelago. Karri trees grow on the slopes far from the main karri forest area. Large trees used to grow there but they have been cut down, and the remaining trees are suffering from fire scorching. The fires encourage invading weeds, like the quake grass in the foreground.

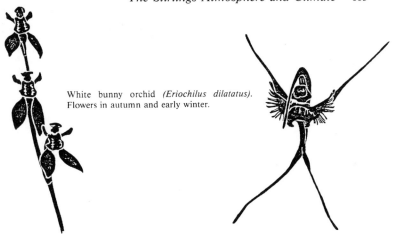

White bunny orchid *(Eriochilus dilatatus).* Flowers in autumn and early winter.

Butterfly orchid *(Caladenia lobata).*

see the bright-yellow pollinia stuck onto it, which pollinates the next flower he visits.

White bunny orchids were flowering in the same area, and hairy leaves of the attractive butterfly orchid were beginning to grow. Further up in the deep shade under wet rocks there were little colonies of round leaved mosquito orchids. Then I noticed a group which was different. They were helmet orchids which have rather odd reddish flowers emerging from their ground-hugging leaf. One wonders what pollinates these orchids? They grow in such wet dark places and flower in mid-winter, so are unlikely to attract anything like bees or wasps. Small midges, probably fungus gnats, are most likely, because they inhabit these places, and are abundant in winter. It is clearly important for the flower to be low down to attract these pollinators because, when the flower is over, something very unusual occurs — the flower stalk grows up to about thirty centimetres, carrying the developing seedhead to the sort of height one would expect the flower to be. Since it grows in such dark places, I wondered whether the deep red flower could emit heat, as arum lilies do, to attract pollinators.

Eventually I came to the head of the gully past dripping moss-covered cliffs with glistening sundews, and then scaled the final rock stack to reach the top. It was one of those rare days when the air clung to the top of the mountain in a dead calm, and it was so quiet that I could still hear the echoing splashes of running water deep in the gullies below, and a chorus of frogs some 500 metres away towards Mt Hassell. A large brightly coloured fly buzzed in the sun overhead, diving on passing insects in the hope of finding a mate. The view was astounding, with the air so clear that the horizon was visible all the way around. The complete range stood out extending from the peaks around Bluff Knoll in the east to Mondurup in the west. The Porongurup Range dominated the southern view, with Mt Manypeaks and Mt Gardner at Two Peoples Bay to the East. Albany and

King George Sound were visible beyond the Porongurups and Mt Frankland could be discerned near Walpole, deep in the karri forest 130 kilometres away. The early morning mist still hung in the air off the range, as small clouds dropped rainbow-clad showers on bushland receding into the distance.

My attention was drawn to some of the rocks on the summit which had corrugated surfaces, exaggerated by the angle of the sunlight, which cast shadows in the hollows between ridges. Looking closely at them gave me a strange feeling, because they corresponded exactly with the sort of ripples one sees in fine sand as the tide goes out on a calm seashore. There was even one where I could see where water seeping out of the sand had run down the shore, breaking through the ripples. I was standing at the top of a mountain 1,051 metres high, well out of the range of seawater nowadays, but the rocks had clearly recorded within them what had happened there over 1,700 million years ago!

The rocks suggest that the large land mass known as the Yilgarn Block, which holds the goldfields area, was bordered by a shallow sea, and as the land eroded, rivers carried sand and silt down to the sea where it was deposited over a long period of time. The sea floor must have slowly sunk down as the material was deposited, maintaining the calm, shallow nature, recording layer after layer of ripple marks and frequent changes of the direction of water currents. The tranquil conditions changed about 1,700 million years ago when severe earth movements began to crush the deposits culminating in the intrusion of the mass of granite 1,100 million years ago, which formed the Porongurups and the Recherche Archipelago. These movements crushed the sand into quartzite and silts into stone and shales. The movements bent the rocks forming the Stirling Range so that the original flat sand now tipped to the south as one can see from the slope of the top of Bluff Knoll.

One of the main assumptions when interpreting geology is that the conditions we observe happening now are the same as those which occurred in the past, and so we can use our observations to interpret what happened when rocks were laid down. Looking at the ripple marks made me wonder whether we should make this assumption, because the conditions were indeed different over 2,000 million years ago. For a start we know that there was no oxygen in the atmosphere — it did not appear until about 1,800 million years ago when cyanobacteria produced so much oxygen that the chemistry of rocks and the atmosphere could absorb no more. I was reminded of a stone I had found in the English Lake District which I treasured for years. It was a strange bubbly rock made of what is known as kidney iron ore. This ore is thought to have been deposited by chemical or biological activity in water during the time when oxygen was being produced, and absorbed by the iron to form layered nodules of iron oxides. The vast deposits of iron ore in the Pilbara were being laid down in shallow lakes at the time as well. In fact there seems to have been an abundance of calm shallow lakes and seas in the early history of the planet. What was the atmosphere like? Perhaps it was much thinner, calm and relatively cloudless, and when rain fell it may have been full of sulphurous acid and hydrogen sulphide. How much water was there? Was there as much then in the early evolution of the planet, or did it slowly build up, or did it come in bursts when each new comet struck the globe? Very slowly we are beginning to piece the jigsaw together and show that things were not always the same. For instance, a recent piece of detective work has shown from the growth of fossil stromatolites in the goldfields that the earth was spinning faster 1,000 million years ago, with 435 days in the year.

What would it have been like standing here 2,000 million years ago? I would have needed a spacesuit to keep out poisonous gases in the atmosphere and a backpack to breathe oxygen. The sky may have been faintly blue from water vapour or even pink in the absence of oxygen and the ground would have appeared totally lifeless, although shaded wet seepages may have had encrusting growths of bacteria. There would have been no ozone layer, so I would have needed a shield to stop ultraviolet radiation reaching my body or eyes, but there may have been enough methane and carbon dioxide in the atmosphere to generate a strong greenhouse effect causing me to be uncomfortably hot. It is interesting that if all the carbon on Earth were in the atmosphere, the temperature would be about 50°C higher than it is now; more like that on the planet Venus.

How will it look in the near future? The clarity of the atmosphere may not last for long. Each time I go back to the U.K. I wince at the atmospheric pollution there. It is amazing that it is tolerated, but I suppose the changes have been slow enough for the majority of the population not to know how fresh and clear the atmosphere could be, and it is convenient for the forces of economics and power-politics to do as little as necessary. Some bureaucrats doggedly maintain that acid rain does not exist, even though the trees and lakes are dying around them. I remember flying to Finland one sunny day in 1969. After years of living with haze and fog I saw the broad band of appalling air pollution heading for southern England from the industrial centres of Europe, and for the first time realised the connection. I had lived through pea-soup fogs from London, but had not appreciated the regional extent of the pollution. It is hard for us in Australia to imagine skies so polluted that one cannot even see up to the clouds overhead, and is only aware of a bland grey envelope. This occurs near London when east winds bring in air which has circulated over Europe.

Smoke control in London got rid of the pea-soup smogs, but clear poisonous gases have replaced them and the industrial activity has grown so much, now, that the pollution covers the entire Northern Hemisphere. America gets it from Japan, England from America, and Siberia from Europe. Do we have to have it in the Southern Hemisphere? One hopes not, but even if we can prevent it, we cannot avoid the other forms of air pollution, which are spreading out from areas of human activity all over the globe. These are changing the global atmosphere, especially carbon dioxide levels, as mentioned in the last chapter, and are changing the climate and resetting the ice age clock.

For a long time it has been suggested that ice ages were caused by minor changes in the Earth's orbit around the sun, but these ideas, known as the Milankovic Model, tended to be laughed at, because the changes in the amount of heat falling on the surface were so minimal. Now these ideas are gaining acceptance, because research on the greenhouse effect provides a very strong scientific basis to account for the large temperature changes. There are three main factors in the Earth's orbit. One is that the Earth is like a spinning toy top — it rotates on its axis at an angle to the sun, but the axis also rotates so that the angle to the sun varies in time. This produces the effect that the tropical zone expands and contracts regularly over a period of about 20,000 years. The other effects are caused by the Earth, like all other planets, having an elliptical orbit around the sun, which changes shape in 100,000 and 400,000 year cycles so that its distance from the sun varies. When these effects are all combined, they produce variations in the heat reaching the surface in a complex pattern which takes millions of years to repeat itself.

It has only recently been possible to accurately measure the temperature changes which have occurred over the last million years or so, using the forms of carbon deposited in foraminifera shells drilled out of the ocean floor. This has shown that there is an uncanny correspondence between the Milankovic Model and temperature changes associated with ice ages. The fact that the latest spate of ice ages started only about a million years ago is explained by South America breaking away from Antarctica at that time, and allowing a circum-polar oceanic current to develop, which stopped water from being circulated into warmer latitudes, and allowed ice to form.

The factors which amplify the effect of small changes in the amount of the sun's energy reaching the ground include the obvious one of ice reflecting energy back into space — so the more ice there is, the greater the amount of energy loss and hence cooling of the planet. (A similar process also helps to prevent overheating in the tropics: the hotter it is, the more cloud is formed which reflects heat back into space.) However, the main climatic factor is the greenhouse effect of gases in the atmosphere, especially carbon dioxide and methane. These gases reduce the amount of heat being reradiated back out into space because, although allowing light to come in, like the glass of a greenhouse, they are opaque to the heat which forms when the light strikes the ground. Without these gases, we would freeze to death every night.

Scientists have been able to find out how the amount of carbon dioxide has varied during the last 20,000 years or so by drilling cores in the Greenland icecap. When snow falls it contains air which becomes trapped as bubbles in the ice. Analysis of these bubbles has shown that there is a sequence of change in the Earth's orbit, followed by increasing carbon dioxide and then a warming of the climate. The reverse takes place at the onset of an ice age, with a change in orbit leading to decreased carbon dioxide and cooling. This suggests that slight temperature changes bring about changes in biological activity which either release more carbon dioxide or absorb more of it. How this occurs is unknown, perhaps it becomes locked in peat during cold times and is released in warmer times? Maybe it gets deposited in limestone, or perhaps methane is involved as well, because there are enormous reserves of this gas which could be released periodically by climatic change. Lowering sea levels or increasing ocean temperatures may allow it to bubble up from the ocean floor, while higher temperatures would release it from the arctic tundra.

However, it is now clear that these factors combine to make small changes in the Earth's orbit into large changes in climate. The disquieting fact is that calculations on the present state of the orbit suggest that we should be going back into an ice age about now — so what has gone wrong? Measurements of atmospheric carbon dioxide may provide the answer; in the last 200 years it has been increasing at an alarming rate caused by the burning of fossil fuels and removal of the world's natural vegetation cover. It has been estimated that in the next fifty years the concentration of carbon dioxide in the atmosphere will be more than the globe has experienced since the time when mankind began evolving from the apes, over 5 million years ago, long before the present spate of ice ages.

Developers and industrialists may be tempted to congratulate themselves on having delayed the onset of the next ice age, but we are now well into uncharted territory. The physical and biological repercussions may be so amplified that we will be powerless to reverse the trend. Data from about 90 million years ago show the Earth's temperature was much warmer than at present, when there was between four and eighteen times as much carbon dioxide in the atmosphere. Something suddenly removed the carbon dioxide in a few thousand years, causing a global cooling of between 8°C and 13°C. The biological consequences of such changes are catastrophic. (A small comfort may be that it suggests that the Earth can cope with enormous changes, and that we can be spared the extreme scenarios exhibited by the planets Mars and Venus — a totally frozen planet, or a runaway greenhouse planet with surface temperatures hot enough to melt lead!) However, it will only take relatively little climatic change to devastate human populations which are still dependent upon "Neolithic" methods of food production.

On my way down the mountain my attention was brought back to the present by some mountain bells. These are very attractive flowers confined to the cooler damper conditions found on the tops of the hills. The Stirling Range has its own flora, like the Barrens in the Fitzgerald River area, which became isolated in the early Tertiary over 40 million years ago. The sea swept inland and virtually surrounded the range, isolating the flora on the island peaks. Now one finds these darwinias with very restricted ranges, some being found only on a group of peaks. Some of the animals are also relics of this time, such as spiders which have probably survived on the tops for millions of years. Snails have also become isolated on the summits, so that they have evolved into separate races or species, and there is also a frog living on the top of Bluff Knoll, which is normally only found in the karri forest near Pemberton.

I drove across the arid plain to the Porongurup Range, past lakes surrounded by the dead skeletons of trees killed by salt running off the surrounding farm country. This range covers only a small area, with the bald-headed tops typical of the south coast granite hills. But here the slopes were covered in thick woodland quite unlike the other hills; this was my first introduction to karri forest. It is a small isolated population, well east of the main area, although there is another even smaller one on Mt Manypeaks. One wonders how long ago the karri forest extended over a much larger area, perhaps stretching to the Stirlings when the frog could have migrated to Bluff Knoll.

If one goes further back in history to before the ice ages, the climate becomes progressively cooler and wetter, and eventually one comes to a time when southern beech forest grew over the area, which is when the spider would have been common. Now conditions are progressively getting less suitable, making the karri forest contract; eventually one may expect it to go the same way as the southern beech forest, and become extinct. I could see that the trees were already looking sick on the Porongurups, being rather small and staggy. The area has now clearly become too dry and fireprone for them to grow as well as they used to. However, it is small isolated populations under intense natural selection, like those at the Porongurups, that eventually lead to new species adapted to local conditions. Studies have shown that this population has already diverged genetically from the karri found in the main area. One wonders how valuable this genetic variation may be in the future. It is possible that these trees may have invaluable adaptations to help to regenerate karri forest in areas which have been subject to excessive fire and drought after modern forest clearance.

I climbed up to one of the tops, and came across a yellow flower growing amongst some large boulders, quite unlike any other I had seen. It was *Villarsia calthifolia*, which only occurs in this small spot; in fact, it is the only known location on the planet. It is incredible to think of the genetic loss now occurring on the planet. This diversity has built up over the 3,800 or so million years that life has existed here, and has had a relatively free run over the last 66 million years to speciate into the staggering complexity found before the Neolithic extermination. Species like this flower are becoming extinct at an unprecedented rate, most before we even know of their existence, like the innumerable species which must have been lost during land clearance in the wheat-belt. I fear that even if we work hard setting aside reserves and growing rare species in botanic gardens, that we will be merely delaying their extinction, because we are not addressing the root cause of the problem, which is the unrelenting progression of land alienation. To have a lasting effect one needs to set in motion something which will reverse the trend, such as finding an economic reason for retaining genetic diversity, demonstrating how useful species are in pharmaceuticals, bio-engineering or in halting the greenhouse effect. But so far these approaches seem to have had little more than a cosmetic effect, because there has been no real move to change the way we manage the planet.

One has to set in motion the new age, the "Post-Neolithic" alga-culture economy, to really change global management. This change would put control of the greenhouse effect well within our grasp, as well as shifting our food production and economy onto a direct reliance on the unlimited incoming solar energy to provide most of our food, energy and materials requirements. With this, and the modern trend to slow our rate of population growth, ecosystems could well begin to regenerate and rebuild into new levels of complexity. Will this little yellow-flowered plant see the day, or is it too late?

Kidney iron ore. This ore was formed deep in the sea as an encrustation. Some think it was produced by encrusting growths of bacteria which deposited the iron in layers, much like in stromatolites. Other workers think it may have been a purely chemical deposition.

9 The Karri Forest: The Changing Role of Forestry

I climbed up a bald granite rock near Albany and looked out over the Southern Ocean. A severe frontal system had passed through during the last few days, and the waves were pounding on the rocks below, creating a salt spray which drifted inland as far as the Stirling Range. A huge albatross passed motionless on the wind, looking like some giant pterosaur. During stormy periods many ocean and Antarctic birds find themselves blown on shore, especially petrels. Scanning the turbulent waters with binoculars I soon picked out a pair of humpbacked whales cruising through the waves. It is marvellous to be able to see these animals around the coast and know that each year they are increasing in numbers, because the Albany Whaling Station is now closed and whaling has ceased in Australian waters.

It is interesting that during the height of the whaling era, some of the most frequent visitors to Australian waters were whaling ships, like the one commanded by Captain Rossiter. He was the one who entertained Eyre in the bay named after him in Cape le Grand National Park. At that time there was no control over the numbers caught, so that the only controls on whaling came from the size of the market for produce and the cost of catching whales. In the heyday whales were a veritable goldmine, with the stock apparently being limitless. As time went on, the size of whales caught became smaller and the most favoured species became so rare that the whalers had to switch to others. To remain economic, the whaling fleets were also pushed into improving their technology so that they could continue to catch enough whales, because they were becoming so scarce. Something had to be done to control the amount of whaling, but this was difficult because the whales were being caught in international waters, and unilateral action by one whaling nation would merely have allowed other countries to catch the remaining stock. The International Whaling Commission was set up and has tried to control whaling, but some countries have continued to operate outside the system and others have exploited loopholes in the agreements.

There was a lot of local opposition to closing the Albany Whaling Station, the last in Australia, but like most other whaling operations it was better closed at a small loss, while people could find other jobs, than continue running until the whale stock was further depleted, possibly to extinction, and end up at the same position later but with an even greater

Red-flowering gum. This widely cultivated tree only grows naturally in a small area on the south coast between Denmark and Walpole.

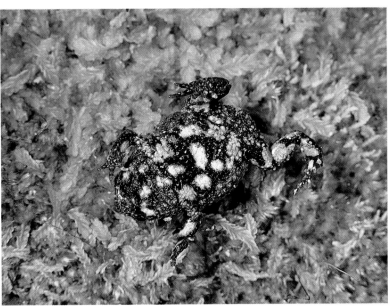

Karri forest frog. This unusual frog *(Metacrinia nichollsi)* is mainly found in the karri forest near the coast, but an isolated population lives on the summit of Bluff Knoll in the Stirling Range. It can be found under rotten logs where it is hard to see because it remains motionless. Its upper surface is black, and when turned over it has orange patches which look like an orange clasp fungus found on the logs.

Valley of the Giants. Red tingle trees *(Eucalyptus jacksonii)* and white-trunked karri *(E. diversicolor)* grow together in this area near Walpole. The relatively high rainfall, even in summer, means that fire rarely burns through this forest, and fire-sensitive animals and plants persist.

Giant trunks left standing like a monument. The huge trees in the karri forest were hard to clear for agriculture. Many ring-barked trunks were left in the early days, much as Neolithic man would have done in early Britain. Much forest country is still being cleared each year by local farmers.

Common dunnart. This little marsupial 'mouse' is common in the karri forest, but like many other mammals takes a long time to return to forests after clear-felling. The introduced house mouse booms into large populations following fires or clear-felling, and is only slowly replaced by native species after many years.

Willy-willy in clear-felled karri forest. Forest management at present uses the technique of total destruction for regeneration. After timber extraction everything is cut down and the area set on fire during the summer. After many years most of the native plants and animals do return, but one wonders how long this sort of practice can continue without the forest changing beyond recognition.

financial loss. The Japanese whaling fleets continued for many years after they began to make losses — the operators finding it easier to cope with small annual losses than face their shareholders with the financial disaster of closing down operations. They continue to take large numbers for "research" purposes in the hope that whaling operations will be allowed to recommence.

It is interesting how the fishing of the oceans continues to operate with the same freedom enjoyed by the early whalers. Yet with the high technology used today, fishing efficiency is very much greater, and very soon many fish will become so rare that they can no longer be fished. The tuna may be one of the first, and as these and other top predators disappear the whole ocean ecology will be altered with unknown consequences. Many countries have difficulty in managing fisheries within their own national boundaries, like the North Sea herrings, so there seems little hope of getting the necessary international agreement to protect the oceans, even though they are such a vital world resource.

When the whales were still being caught at Albany, white pointer sharks used to come and feed on the corpses, causing local big-game hunters to go out and kill them. It is interesting how support has grown to save the whales, but little sympathy seems to be generated for the shark, which may well be in greater danger of extinction. These sharks live to a great age — well over a hundred years — and may only produce a few young in their lifetime, so their numbers can be very quickly depleted by hunting. The number of people killed by sharks is incredibly low, probably not very different from deaths related to whales, yet people seem to get great satisfaction out of killing sharks. Fortunately views are changing about large predators, and "big-game hunters" are now using cameras instead of guns on lions and tigers, so perhaps the shark's turn will come. They have been here a lot longer than we have — over 400 million years longer — so perhaps should be treated with appropriate respect.

Driving west along the coast road, I turned off to go to the Walpole/Nornalup National Park. I passed green paddocks full of cattle, and areas of scrub bulldozed ready for burning, before coming to the low-lying, undulating coastal part of the park, which was ablaze with colour. The swampy parts were thick with tall orange, tassel-like flowerheads of swamp bottlebrush, while the rises had rather stumpy, gnarled gum trees laden with a variety of flowers ranging from orange to deep crimson. This is one of the very few places where the red-flowering gum (*Eucalyptus ficifolia*) grows naturally. It grows along a small section of the south coast, in which much of the land has already been cleared or is in the process of being cleared, so relatively little remains under protection. However, the future of the species seems to be well assured, because it is widely grown as a street tree, not only in Australia but in many other parts of the world. This is not so with the many insects and other invertebrates which are dependent on the natural coastal thickets of these gum trees. All plants have a variety of insects which are dependent on them, and the red-flowering gum is unlikely to be an exception. But we know so little about the natural ecology of the thickets that many species may become extinct before we know anything about them, just as if it were a piece of tropical rainforest.

Driving inland the wind and salt-trimmed coastal scrub gave way to taller, staggy trees which rose higher and higher until I had to crane my neck to see the canopies above, atop column-like trunks. This was in the Valley of the Giants, where red tingle trees (*Eucalyptus jacksonii*) grow. They persist here because the climate is the closest in Western Australia to the wet conditions of the Tertiary times, when cool temperate forests grew and summer fires were rare. The area has as much as 300 mm rainfall during the summer months, with a total of 1,200 mm per annum. The red tingle trees have a shaggy, reddish-brown bark which contrasts with the gleaming smooth trunks of the karri trees. They grow to a great age, with some having enormous trunks up to five metres in diameter and twenty metres in circumference. Two smaller kinds of tingle are also restricted to this area.

Careful searching in the leaf litter yields some of the animal survivors from the days of the great southern beech forests. A tiny spider, which has no means of avoiding fire, builds its fragile web between fallen leaves in the damp rotting leaf litter. Its relatives thrive in cool beech forests in Tasmania and South America. During the summer of 1987 a huge fire was started, which swept through much of this part of the south coast, roaring through a section of the tingle forest. The canopy was completely scorched and I found the blackened trunks were now clothed with new green growth, and the ground covered with a dense thicket of vegetation growing up in the unaccustomed light. I wonder how long it will be before the spider can recolonise the burned area, or will fires now sweep the area too frequently for it to persist at all?

I drove through the forest and came out into agricultural land again. In some places the landowners had not got around to removing the final remnants of the original majestic forest. I stopped to watch a farmer cutting hay in his pennyroyal-scented, butterfly-filled pasture, reminiscent of the English countryside. He was winding his machine through a henge-like monument of forty-metre trunks, left standing and starkly reminding one of what stood there only a few decades ago. Neolithic people would have left trunks standing like this as they cleared the original English lowland valley forest. They left none of the forest for us to see today, leaving only lifeless monuments instead, like Stonehenge. Can we do better?

The road went back into the forest and I came to the foot of Mt Frankland, which I had seen from Toolbrunup in the Stirling Range. Climbing through a forest of karri trees I found a wide variety of flowers: clematis, blue dampieras, mats of boomerang trigger plants, and dandelion-like smooth cats-ear which is a widespread invader from Neolithic England. From the top the air was still clear enough to see the Porongurups and as far as the Stirling Range. Forest stretched below in all directions, with patches of white-trunked karri, dark marri and staggy jarrah trees marking different soils and drainage conditions, while the swampy sides of creeks were marked by bullich, another white-trunked gum tree. But the view to the south-west was masked by columns of smoke rising from the advancing agricultural edge, which is still gnawing away at the dwindling primeval forest. Land owners were burning off the latest areas they had bulldozed to extend their pastures.

Continuing from Walpole towards Pemberton I saw a roadside sign warning of logging trucks. The road re-entered primeval vegetation where the low-lying areas were almost flat and covered in swampy heath with a rich mixture of bottlebrushes — melaleucas, beaufortias, callistemons and a host of myrtles, while the ground was covered in a rich assortment of trigger plants and other small plants. The poor nature of the soil encouraged insect-eating plants with a wide variety of sundews and bladderworts. I was also lucky enough to find an Albany pitcher plant — these are very interesting because they show how evolution can lead plants to independently arrive at a common structure. The pitchers on pitcher plants are very efficient insect traps, designed so that insects are attracted to them and fall in. The best designs include: an attractive secretion, a lid, a waxy side to make the insect slip into the liquid at the base and a lip to prevent it escaping once it has fallen in. Several plants have evolved almost identical pitchers even though they come from quite unrelated origins. The Albany pitcher plant is unique, belonging to a family all on its own, but with flowers resembling those of the saxifrages.

The ridges rose up from the swamps with stunted staggy jarrah/marri forest, which grew taller at the top, making the ridges more conspicuous. Rounding a bend, I had to swerve onto the gravel at the roadside to avoid a log-truck speeding like some huge, unstoppable juggernaut, appearing intent on destroying everything in its path. The trees grew larger as I travelled further, with the road passing through patches of karri, and the landscape becoming scarred by logging roads reminiscent of some I had seen in Borneo, where they looked like drainage channels from the air — draining the life out of the forest. Rounding another bend I entered the first tall karri forest with the gleaming trunks arching over the road like some gigantic marble cathedral. I slowed to take in this awe-inspiring scene, much to the annoyance of other travellers preoccupied by other demands, but the experience was over all too quickly and I was back out into the swampy flats again. However, each succeeding ridge brought me into an even more impressive stand of karri trees, quite unbelievable to those accustomed to the puny oaks and beeches of Europe. These karris are among the tallest trees in the world; the largest measuring ninety metres, with the first branches often fifty or sixty metres above the ground.

I went along a track into the forest near Pemberton, well away from the main road, and walked amongst the trees. It is an incredible feeling, looking up and seeing the trunks converging into the canopy high above, and hearing a seething birdlife somewhere up there, screeching like distant cicadas. After peering for a long time one adapts to the perspective and realises that what appear to be flying insects are in fact lorikeets dashing between flower-laden boughs high overhead. After a while my neck began to ache; it was like looking up to see the stars at night, so I lay down on the ground to have a more relaxed view of the canopy. The air was breathless on the forest floor, yet a gentle roar, like distant breakers, came from high overhead as a gentle breeze caressed the treetops. Nearer at hand, at the level of normal trees, there are other layers of foliage, from peppermints and karri oak (a casuarina with an oak-like grain). Then, under them, are the broad-leaved karri hazel, which have large hazel-like leaves at first, changing to a smaller leaf as they get older. Then there are white- and yellow-flowered wattle bushes, purple hoveas and bracken growing over a ground cover of irises, trigger plants, orchids and mosses. The orchids include many helmet, mosquito and slipper orchids.

Boomerang triggerplant. The flowers are arranged in such a way that insects are unable to learn ways of approaching the flower without tripping the trigger mechanism.

One is so dwarfed by the dimensions of this environment that one cannot help feeling that one's true place is merely an insignificant part of a huge biological whole. We share so much with the life on Earth that we are totally dependent upon its continued existence. Our origins can be traced in the trees, plants and animals around us; in the way our cells live and grow, and in the fragments of DNA and mitochondria that we share with them from our common ancestry. It is in places such as this that one can feel the common force of life, which requires that the world's natural ecology remains in harmony if we are to continue to enjoy all the food, water and air we need. Yet we seem to act as if we were invaders from outer-space, exploiting whatever we find useful until nothing remains and we move on to the next planet. This attitude goes back to our ancestry when populations were under natural biological control. It was probably sustainable into the time of shifting agriculture of the early Neolithic, when people could move to new pastures each time the soil became nutrient-deficient. It is untenable today, with the world population causing the total destruction of natural ecosystems. We will indeed have to become space-travellers and move to other planets or live in artificial biospheres, unless we can extricate ourselves from our Neolithic way of thinking.

I followed a kangaroo track which wound through beard heath and hibbertia shrubs, and past dripping bracken fronds. I disturbed a nest of ants thronging over its heap of casuarina leaves, much like the pine-needle nests of wood-ants in England. I began to wonder what animals would have lived here before mankind arrived in Australia. Lumbering diprotodons and giant kangaroos perhaps, hunted by marsupial lions and thylacines. There would have been koalas living in the south-west then — could they have climbed the karri trees? Perhaps the trunks evolved their tall, slippery nature to prevent leaf-eating mammals like the koala from climbing them. These visions then became greyed by a sense of impending doom; I became aware of a faint smell of smoke in the air, and an unnatural light in the undergrowth ahead.

I pushed on and breaking through a screen of hazel leaves came upon a scene of unspeakable destruction. The karri forest was gone, and in its place was a jumble of charred limbs and stumps surrounded by white ash, while a blue smoke haze shimmered over the hot ground. It was just as if the area had been cleared for agriculture. As I surveyed the scene, dazed by the enormity of it all, a willy-willy sprang up in the heated air, and swept over to embrace me in an obscene, macabre dance, partnered by phantoms of ash and singed leaves. It was like experiencing the nightmarish scene depicted in "Valse Triste", by the Finnish composer Sibelius, of a dying woman desperately trying to dance with passing wispy figures before Death knocks at the door.

Here were some of the practical consequences of modern state-of-the-art, science-backed, high-tech forestry. The scientists and technicians behind this scene represent the peak of forestry today. They have gone through similar training to those who are in charge of managing forests throughout the world, and they are being sent, with international help, to advise on the management of the Amazonian and South-East Asian forests. The scene I witnessed made me wonder about this advice. Could it be worse for the local ecosystems than no advice at all? What is the basis of this thinking? What assumptions are being made? Probably mainly that forestry is the science which provides the best management of land for timber production, and hence forests are merely areas of land which have been designated for this purpose. The science is about timber extraction, regeneration and maintaining a sustainable yield, the control of pests and weeds, fire hazard reduction, of productivity, economics, employment and politics. This is what all the research is about, and is the reason for clear-felling and burning; apparently karri trees regenerate best with this treatment, and it is cheaper and easier to log even-aged stands of trees.

Of course karri forest as we know it will not return, it will be secondary forest, somewhat nutrient-depleted and impoverished. This does not seem to be regarded as important, because the forest is all to be felled again before it has had time to grow into large trees as we have now. One wonders how sustainable this process may be. Coppicing has gone on for at least a thousand years over the rich English soils without obvious signs of increasing degradation (although nothing remains of the original forest), but Australian soils are well-known to be highly susceptible to degradation. Could it be that there is a British way-of-thinking present, which assumes karri soils can go on producing karri indefinitely? Could it be that much of the soil fertility is hauled out with the trees in a similar way to that of tropical rainforests? We have not been here long enough to have the necessary long-term data. Perhaps we will find that karri will not grow the third or fourth time around.

The tree-felling reminded me of the whaling industry; there initially seemed to be an endless supply of trees, but more wood is still being extracted than grows each year so that the trees to be removed are to be younger, and timber workers are seeking ways of using more of the wood they cut. They are also beginning to use trees which used to be discarded, such as marri. These are all the symptoms of a declining "fishery" known to any ecology student. It seems as if our forests cannot sustain the rate of extraction we are allowing now, so when is it to end? Which human generation is going to pay for it? Is this the sensible management we are trying to impose on developing countries?

I began to think about my own contacts with forestry. My first job was at the Forestry Commission Research Station at Alice Holt in England, where I met a dedicated group of workers doing research on growing trees, and methods of protecting them from pests and diseases. Many of these workers had been through a training which for many years provided graduates for all the colonies. Forestry in England had a strongly agricultural approach, because in the 1920s the country was so denuded of wood that something had to be done for strategic purposes in case of another war. The Forestry Commission was set up to plant millions of trees, and any land not under agriculture was open to forestry — commons, heaths, bogs, woodland, downs and moors. These were all the most valuable areas for retaining England's fauna and flora, but this was not the concern of the Forestry Commission. It had its job to do: the land was bought or leased and science was used to the full to turn it as efficiently as possible into economic forest. The land was bulldozed, drained, burned, fertilised, fenced, planted, thinned, sprayed with herbicides or insecticides and otherwise managed purely for tree production. The brief was to plant quick-growing trees, and millions of pounds were spent in doing just that — no return was expected until the trees began to mature. But now the government is wondering what to do with its expensive forests. One is reminded of a similar but less extensive operation begun in 1805, during the Napoleonic wars, when oak trees were planted for building battleships, because wars had created a serious shortage of suitable timber. Alice Holt Forest was planted and ready for use by about 1915; but by then the ships were made of iron.

I came into closer contact with the Forestry Commission forests anew when I became responsible for the Nature Reserves in the East Anglian Breckland. This area was one of the first to be cleared by Neolithic people about 6,000 years ago, because its pine forests on light soil were easier to destroy than lime/oak forest on heavy soils. Thousands of years of grazing and agriculture, together with rabbit plagues (another consequence of William the Conqueror), made much of the area into a semi-desert with inland sand-dunes. The long-term human habitation of the area meant that, in spite of its desert-like features, it had had thousands of years to evolve new ecosystems. Only little remained of this ecosystem, because most of the area had been planted with an exotic species of pine, which is partly why the reserves were so important. The Forestry Commission had also tried to drain some of the few swamplands, fortunately without success because these areas have proved incredibly valuable in telling us about the prehistory of the area, from the ice age to the Neolithic land-clearance. This history can all be traced in the pollen grains contained in peat.

Later, when I returned to work on squirrels with the cooperation of Forestry Commission workers, I began to notice a change. Economic facts were beginning to erode the foundations of the organisation, because it was becoming clear that the Commission was going to remain a costly encumbrance for the government as far as could be seen into the future. Bureaucracies change very slowly. However, the writing was on the wall and reasons were being sought for the continued existence of the Forestry Commission. Its role in wildlife conservation was advanced as a reason for retaining the forests; after all, the pine forests encouraged a few pine-loving species, such as red squirrels and crossbills. Management objectives also became more diversified, so that where deer control was too costly, the forests were managed to produce venison instead of timber. Forestry training programs changed with the times and provided excellent courses in wildlife management and conservation. But the inevitable seems to be happening now, plain economics have caught up with the Commission, and have taken precedence over everything else — the forests are being sold off to private interests.

The whole exercise has made an enormous impact on Britain's ecology, removing a large percentage of the country's dwindling ecosystems, all of which were the culmination of thousands of years of traditional human usage. It was like taking a bulldozer to the country's ancient cities and towns, knocking down their cathedrals and cottages, and replacing them with a geometric arrangement of modern concrete and glass office blocks.

I have been an interested observer in Australia, seeing similar trends going through the Forests Department, now called the Department of Conservation and Land Management (CALM), which is responsible for forestry, national parks, nature reserves, and wildlife research. I was very fearful some years ago that the economic argument would lead to more areas of forest being released for agriculture, but the current problems with salt, loss of rainfall, concern about conservation and the global environment make this unlikely to occur on a large scale. However, the increasing use of the conservation argument for retaining forests is a concern, because there is a risk that a government will find that it can no longer justify the cost of managing such a large conservation area, and it will succumb to the attraction of a once-off windfall profit. The land could be released for timber and woodchipping demands, or to some form of privatisation, despite the long-term value of the forests to the community in the form of tourism, recreation and conservation.

I think the question of economics will answer itself as time goes on. The forests are a world resource needed to preserve the world environment, as well as for everyone to enjoy. Alternatives to wood-pulp paper, woodchips and natural forest-grown timber will eventually have to be found. There is already a need for this because of a world shortage, so one can imagine the situation in the near future, with increased world affluence and declining forests. What will happen when the population of Australia is, say, 50 million? What chance is there going to be of enough timber then, if there is not enough now?

Welcome moves are ahead to make paper out of sugarcane waste, and there is hope from the huge areas of agricultural land being planted with various gum trees in response to land degradation problems and fears of the greenhouse effect. This is where the foresters' skills are urgently needed; not in the remaining areas of "wildwood". These workers are ideally prepared for growing trees as an agricultural crop on land already degraded by agriculture. The world is crying out for them to use these skills, together with their more recently acquired background knowledge of wildlife management and conservation, to manage this process of revegetation and reconstruction.

In the future I hope that paper will be one of the products made by alga-farms, using genetically engineered bacteria to make cellulose fibres. This is when Australian and world tourists will marvel at what we have kept of the remaining karri forests. They will be open-mouthed on hearing how long we went on cutting the trees down, and incredulous that some of the wood should have been used for woodchips. The karri forest is a natural heritage which belongs to the world of the future, like the Amazon Basin, and we have no right to go on cutting it for selfish, short-term economic gains.

Karri cedar or wattie *(Agonis juniperina)*. Grows bordering rivers and swamps in the karri forest. It often remains after land clearance, growing into attractive trees. It is host to a kind of native aphid, like its relative the peppermint tree.

The Warren River. This river meanders through the karri forest with its tea-coloured waters rich with marron and other aquatic life. It is bordered by wattie trees and behind one can see large marri trees which grow to a massive size in this area.

Swamp bottlebrush *(Beaufortia sparsa)*. Flowers profusely in summer from January until April. It grows in swamps between Margaret River and Albany.

Marron. These huge freshwater crayfish inhabit the snag-strewn rivers and creeks of the karri forest. They are only available to license-holding amateurs, but even so have been heavily over-fished. Fishing has been banned from time to time to allow the stock to increase.

Enchanted forest. A paperbark swamp near the mouth of the Donnelly River which has curiously distorted trunks.

Basalt cliffs at Black Point. This rock was formed as lava flowing from a volcano during the Cretaceous. The rock is present over the region as far as Bunbury. The outcrop here is hexagonally jointed like that seen by Joseph Banks when he sailed for Iceland past Fingal's Cave in the Hebrides.

Sunset catching the skeletal remains of a majestic tree. Much of the forest was saved in the early days because the cost of clearing these huge trees was too great. But the soil in most of the karri forest is suitable for agriculture, and there is little incentive for landowners to retain forest on their land. Licenses to clear are still being readily granted in much of the south-west.

10 Mammoth Cave: Rising Sea Levels

There is an area on the Warren River between Pemberton and the coast which is particularly dear to me. I have spent many happy hours walking through its pennyroyal-scented meadows under the shade of karri cedars, or going through peppermint-covered slopes into the surrounding marri and karri forest. Other times I have sat on a log, idly watching the tea-stained water as it drifts over the sandy bottom, past fallen trees and into deep black marron pools.

On one such day I amused myself looking at the animal life by the river. There were damselflies, perched motionless on twigs, with diaphanous wings outstretched, and a river dragonfly basking on a fallen log. Small caddis flies floated through the air like winged seeds, and mayflies with long tails zigzagged over the surface of the water. I noticed a cranefly on a wet log at the water's edge, which on closer examination proved not to be a cranefly at all, but a very primitive tanyderid relation (*Radinoderus occidentalis*). This family has wings very similar to those of fossils found in Permian rocks, which belonged to the earliest flies known. The wing veins of these flies are very close to those of scorpion-flies, and it is thought that some Permian scorpion-flies must have lost the hind pair of wings and become the first true fly. This novel development started the evolutionary pathway which led to all the flies populating the world today. These tanyderid flies are rarely

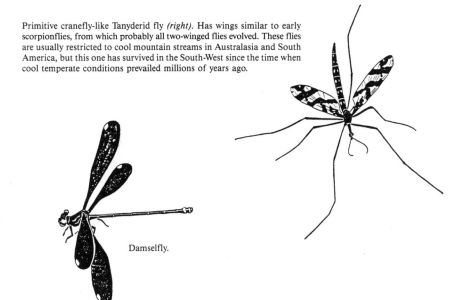

Primitive cranefly-like Tanyderid fly *(right)*. Has wings similar to early scorpionflies, from which probably all two-winged flies evolved. These flies are usually restricted to cool mountain streams in Australasia and South America, but this one has survived in the South-West since the time when cool temperate conditions prevailed millions of years ago.

Damselfly.

encountered now, usually only after patient searching beside cool mountain streams in Australia and South America. This species is only found in the extreme south-west of Western Australia, and is unusual because it lives where there are no cool mountain streams.

The discovery of this fly made me look more closely at the other insects, wondering whether they have some unusual features as well, reflecting the geological history of the continent. Perhaps one could find evidence of the time over 40 million years ago when the whole of Australia was covered in cool temperate rainforest, and southern beech predominated in the south-west, where there were many permanent cold rivers and streams. The damselfly has certainly been here a very long time, having no close relatives in the rest of Australia, and the same applies to most of the cold-water dragonflies, two of which belong to genera unique to the south-west. The

Hovering dragonfly. Unlike most other insects, dragonflies wings beat alternately with the first pair out of phase with the second. Other insects have the wings linked so that they beat together. Huge early relatives of the dragonflies flew in the Carboniferous over 300 million years ago, long before there were any other aerial predators, or even spiders webs (spiders did not learn to build webs until the early Cretaceous 160 million years later).

remaining aquatic insects, including the caddis flies, mayflies, stoneflies and alderflies, also show that they have been isolated in the south-west for a very long time, with many unique species. They are mostly cool temperate species, related to those which prefer mountain streams and beech forests in the south-east. They also include some which show affinities with species found in New Zealand and South America, and so must share a common origin, when all the countries were united in the great southern continent of Gondwanaland.

A large snag had some broken mussel shells on it where a water-rat had been feeding, and I looked into the water where I could see tracks made by mussels dragging themselves across the sandy bottom. A small marron was busying itself, probing in the sand for insect larvae. It is remarkable how successful freshwater crayfish are in Australia. I remember the excitement when I first found crayfish in England, at a time when they had already become rare through disturbance of waterways and pollution. They are now extinct in most of the country, and they are also dying out on the continent of Europe, where they are attacked by a fungal disease which possibly takes hold in animals weakened by aluminium released into the water by acid rain. The Australian species belong to quite different genera of crustaceans, and five species are known in Western Australia, including the yabbie, which has been introduced from the East. The marron is the largest, and is as big as the European lobster.

Unfortunately the marron is not proving as easy to culture as the yabbie, because it has a cannibalistic streak. Like all crustaceans and insects, it has to moult its skin to grow, at which time it becomes quite soft until the new skin hardens. If kept in dense culture ponds the animals which have shed their skins are quickly eaten. Research has yielded ways of reducing this problem, such as trying to reproduce an environment similar to a snag-strewn river, using a honeycomb-like reef of material for the animals to hide in while they are vulnerable. Old motor car tyres have proved to be quite useful for reef-building, but the crustaceans still have to be protected from other predators such as water-rats, long-necked turtles and herons.

After a very pleasant day in this environment, with the families occupied catching marron, we had a feast fit for royalty, sitting around the campfire under the stars. We talked of this and that, sipping good wines and cracking the last claws, when a strange feeling slowly impinged on my consciousness. Something very odd was going on — but what? My eyes were drawn away from the social gathering to the starlit sky. That was it! Instead of the usual black backdrop to the stars, the whole sky was patterned in wispy figures of green and pink, which slowly evolved and regrouped into new shapes as I watched. Was it overindulging in marron? Surely not Don's wine! But the others looked up and, yes, they could see it as well. It was one of those rare occasions when the southern aurora can be seen as far north as Australia; normally it is restricted to much higher latitudes. It was lucky that we were sitting out under the stars at the right moment to see it.

Space research has yielded much more information on the aurora than was known a few years ago. It is associated with activity on the sun, which goes through an eleven-year sunspot cycle. During the peak of sunspot activity enormous magnetic storms occur, stringing huge solar flares high above its surface. The massless electro-magnetic radiation from these flares reaches us within eight minutes, travelling at the speed of light, but much of the energy in the flare is released as charged particles, which cannot travel as fast and take a day or so to reach the Earth. As they approach Earth they strike its magnetic field, which deflects them to the poles where they hit atoms in the upper atmosphere, releasing some of their energy as light. Mostly we only become aware of this activity when it interferes with radio and television reception, but the particles also have an effect on satellites. The particles heat the upper atmosphere, expanding air into the orbits of satellites so that they slow down and fall towards Earth. Weaker streams of these particles leave the sun all the time as the "solar wind" which deflect the tails of comets making them stream away from the sun.

It is extraordinary how we take the sun for granted; here we are, basking in its light and heat, mindless of its nature. Yet it is a vast ball of intense nuclear activity and wracked by unbelievable forces. It is incredible to think that such an active body should be so unchanging; it is such a reliable source of energy that little has changed during the whole period of the evolution of life, and it seems as if we can indeed take it for granted. But variations do occur, such as the sunspot cycle, which affect us more than was thought in the past. For a long time it has been believed that weather is affected by the cycle, with tree growth rings showing some correlation with an eleven-year cycle, and some animal populations seem to run in similar cycles. However, weather is such a complex phenomenon that changes are hard to correlate with any single cause. Recent work has shown that sunspots change the direction of flow of air in the upper atmosphere which undoubtedly influences weather. Also it has been possible to make accurate comparison of global temperature records, which clearly show average temperatures rise by as much as one degree during periods of sunspot activity. Another study has found that sunspot activity is not as regular and dependable as was originally thought, there being a period of 100 years or so in the sixteenth century when there were no sunspots. This is when the Little Ice Age struck Europe: the river Thames was frozen over in London, and fairs and winter games took place in the middle of the river.

Sunspot activity is clearly going to have an influence on global weather patterns, and may double the effect of greenhouse gases at sunspot peaks. It may become particularly important to predict unusual changes in sunspot activity, such as that associated with the Little Ice Age, and research workers will be looking for long-term fossil records of solar activity. These could be found in deep ocean sediments or in strongly layered rocks, such as the banded iron formations found in the Pilbara and the goldfields, where they have already been identified.

The party grew quiet, taking in the external phenomenon and the night became so silent that one could hear the distant roar of the ocean breakers ten kilometres away. Some time later we took a forest track south towards the mouth of the Warren River, through scrub and over marri-covered consolidated sand-dunes, until we came to a wall of sand towering over the trees. Climbing up the side was hard work, slipping down half a step for every one up, until we came to the canopies of trees drowning under the advancing dune front. Once at the top we looked out over the Sahara-like sand-desert of the Yeagerup Dunes. Most of the wide coastal plain here is made up of consolidated sand dunes with duneslack swamps in between. The sand is so light that it does not take much to start a blow-out, such as grazing cattle or burning the vegetation, and once started the strong winds in the area make the mobile sand grow and engulf everything in its path. The only coastal settlement in the area, Windy Harbour, records the nature of the country.

The huge volumes of sand are of great interest to mining companies, because they contain mineral sands. The sand all comes from the breakdown of rocks, originally being the crystals in igneous rocks such as granites and basalts, although some shell sand is present in places, coming from the remains of animal life in the sea. As the rocks weather, those minerals which react with water and acid decompose into clays and salts and are washed away into lakes and the sea. The remaining minerals, mostly made up of a residue of quartz, but including crystals of rare minerals, are left behind.

In the course of time the sand is blown by the wind or carried by rivers and deposited in the sea, near the shoreline. The waves on the shore continually sweep the sand along with them, sorting the sand according to size of grain and its density, like a prospector panning for gold. Tides come and go, sea levels rise and fall, and sand dunes are formed and inundated, so that the whole sandmass is continually sorted and re-sorted until rare crystals are collected into workable mineral deposits. The important minerals are the black coloured ilmenite, an oxide of iron and titanium, and the usually brownish rutile which is titanium dioxide. Also found are monazite containing rare earth elements (cerium, lanthanum, erbium, yttrium, etc.) with thorium, and the mineral zircon (zirconium silicate).

The titanium minerals are particularly valuable for paints, and for aircraft construction, where a lightweight metal with a very high melting point is required, such as for the nose of supersonic aircraft. Deposits are being worked at Capel and Eneabba, and more mines are planned in the Scott River area, near Augusta. Australia is one of the main sources of these minerals, but because the sources are often coastal, some valuable wilderness areas grow over large mineral deposits, such as Fraser Island in Queensland. Monazite poses one of the major problems of working these deposits, because it contains the radioactive element thorium, which makes it difficult to safely dispose of waste from mineral-sand workings.

Our next excursion was further west along a sandtrack into D'Entrecasteaux National Park, past low-lying land with flowering swamp bottlebrushes and strandlines showing how impassable the land is during winter when the road may be deep under water. As it was, the car became stuck in the sand at one point and had to be towed out by a larger 4WD. After going through many dunes and swamps we eventually came over a rise, and through some peppermints and coastal wattles, to see the shore stretched out before us near Black Point. We could see breakers crashing over black pavement-like rocks and into a sandy bay. A closer look at the rocks showed that they had an extraordinary regular structure, just like those in the Giant's Causeway in Ireland, or Fingal's Cave in the Hebrides seen by Joseph Banks on his way to Iceland. The black rock is cracked into a regular six-sided honeycomb structure so that it appears as if one is walking on hexagonal paving stones. The cliff at the other end of the beach was made up of organ-pipe-like columns of the rock, twenty metres high.

The rock comes from a basalt lava flow which took place in the early Cretaceous period, about 110 million years ago. Basalt lava flows rapidly, almost like water, and can spread out from a volcano to cover a large area, like those in Hawaii today. The lava flow which formed these rocks was very extensive, spreading from Black Point to as far as Bunbury — in fact it is known as the Bunbury Basalt. No sign of the original volcano is known; it may have been covered by later sediments on the Australian mainland, or conceivably by the ice on Antarctica. The early Cretaceous was an active time for this area, because Australia was breaking away from Antarctica, and movement was taking place along the Darling Fault which runs south from Perth and out to sea near Black Point. These turbulent geological events could have resulted in the volcanic activity of the area.

As it is relatively thin, the lava cools too quickly for large crystals to form. In time, with expansion and contraction due to changes in temperature and the percolation of moisture, stresses build up which cause the rock to crack, rather like mud in a dried-up pond. It seems as if the cracks start as parallel splits along the edge, but as they slowly work their way into the body of the rock they become more random, cutting across one another until they sort themselves out into the geometric pattern which best accommodates the contracting rock. This happens to be in the form of a hexagonal honeycomb.

Walking along the sandy shore I could see a surface layer of black sand being swept by waves over the light coloured quartz sand of the beach, and collecting where there was least wave movement. This was presumably some ilmenite washed out of the basalt rock, and was being processed by the waves to form some future mineral sand deposit. Under the waves I could see ripples in the sand, just like those I had seen fossilised in the rocks on Toolbrunup in the Stirlings, dating from similar wave actions nearly 2,000 million years ago.

The basalt reminded me of the huge basalt flow in the Drakonsberg Mountains in South Africa, where a particularly violent geological event led to the formation of the gold and diamond deposits in that country, and I wondered whether this area between Augusta and the Darling Fault could prove to have a particularly interesting geology. Much of the rock is now buried under Cretaceous and Tertiary sediments, but it must have been subject to a violent period as Australia split away from Antarctica. Curiously enough, this may be linked with the frequency with which whales beach themselves in the area, because it appears that whales use magnetic lines of force to navigate at sea. Anomalies caused by unusual rock formations could give false information and lead them on to the beaches.

The next port of call was on the Leeuwin Block. This is a curious ridge of rock running from Cape Leeuwin to Cape Naturaliste (Augusta to Dunsborough). The rocks are very old and metamorphosed, but it is not known whether they have any relationship with the main goldfields Yilgarn Block, forty-eight kilometres away. The Dunsborough and Darling Faults define the edges of the two blocks, and there could have been a rift valley between, formed as Gondwanaland broke up. Permian rocks fill the base of the valley, known as the Bunbury Trough, so the rift may have occurred at about the time the Indian subcontinent was splitting away from Australia and the Leeuwin Block could have been a part of India, but was left behind while the rest headed off for the Northern Hemisphere.

I was interested in much more recent events associated with deep sand-dune formations. The sand blown up onto the west coast seems to have contained much more shell-sand than that found on the south coast, possibly because the warmer water allowed shell-forming marine organisms to flourish. This has meant that instead of remaining loose and potentially mobile as on the south coast, the dunes of the west turn into limestone, as mentioned in Chapter 1. The amount of rainfall may also be significant, because the more rain the more rapidly the lime is leached from the soil. This leaching process has had a particularly dramatic effect on the deep limestones along the Leeuwin Ridge, creating a series of caves and gorges.

Approaching the caves I passed through jarrah/marri forest, and then into a patch of karri forest, which was like those on the Porongurups and Mt Manypeaks in that it was so far away from the main karri forest area around Pemberton. Coming to Mammoth Cave reminded me of limestone caves I had visited in England, such as Wookey Hole in Somerset. The interest in the caves has similar origins, because they were used by people in the ice ages, and can tell us a great deal about the prehistory of the area, going back over 37,000 years. A few engravings found in the nearby Devil's Lair bear an incredible similarity to works by Old Stone-Age (Palaeolithic) Magdalenian people in Europe. Of course the "mammoth" bones of the cave were not mammoths, but large extinct marsupials, like diprotodons and giant kangaroos.

A considerable amount of patient work has been done on the deposits in the caves to try and unravel the course of prehistory. This has not been easy, because cave deposits are not neatly laid down in layers, but tend to become jumbled by people and animals digging holes and scuffing the material about the cave floor. The age of the deposits also goes back beyond that for which radiocarbon dating can be used, so anything older than 37,000 years can only be roughly aged. It has been found that the prehistoric environment had a rich variety of animal life, with several species of giant kangaroos, an ox-sized diprotodon, wombats, koalas, marsupial lions, thylacines, tasmanian devils, and giant echidnas. There were also many others which still existed in Australia when the Europeans first came to settle, such as rock wallabies, bettongs, potoroos, and hare wallabies.

There is a continuing argument as to whether hunter-gatherer people were responsible for the extinction of so many species throughout the world, or whether this was caused by rapid weather changes associated with ice ages. Probably it was a combination of the two, as the last and most severe ice age coincided with the rapid invasion and build-up of world human populations and technological innovations which yielded ever more deadly weapons. Thus many of the large mammals were already gone by the time Europeans came, and others only needed changes wrought by European agriculture and introduced species to join them on the extinct list. The Californian tar pits show a similar extinction associated with mankind — but it could be that the weather changes were the root cause favouring mankind and disadvantaging the large mammals.

A more detailed analysis of the cave deposits provides us with some information which may become particularly relevant over the next fifty years or so. The animals found in the cave deposits show variations over the years which suggest changes in the vegetation surrounding the caves. The most obvious changes are the appearance of honey possums and rock wallabies as the last ice age started and their loss during the warmer period after the ice age. Both these species are associated with more open heathy conditions, confirming the greater aridity of Australia during the last ice age. When the forest returned, particularly when karri forest became established, these species would have disappeared from the area. Human artefacts also show interesting changes, especially the appearance of chert tools made from rocks not known in the area. These probably came from a quarry now well out to sea; the seashore having been as much as thirty-five kilometres further west than it is now.

As time goes on more and more data are being collected to show the drastic changes which have occurred in the past. Not only the climatic changes, but the enormous fluctuations in sea-level that have directly affected animals, plants and people living in coastal regions. We live in a time when the sea level has been remarkably static for the last 6,000 years, and we tend to think that this will continue indefinitely, but looking into the past gives quite a different perspective, suggesting that a Noah-like flood is a distinct possibility. From 17,000 to 6,000 years ago the sea advanced thirty-five kilometres, particularly during the 2,000 years 10-12,000 years ago. Much of this movement is attributed to the melting of polar ice caps, but in fact only small temperature changes in the ocean are sufficient to cause considerable changes in sea level, due to the expansion of water. We must remember that we are still well within a period of glaciation, even though we are in what is known as an interglacial period. The world still has vast areas of cold seas and huge volumes of water locked up in the polar ice caps. If carbon dioxide levels increased to the levels found in the early Cretaceous, the ice age would come to an end, and the sea would advance over the Nullarbor again, and turn the Leeuwin Block into a chain of offshore rocky islets.

Current projections suggest that in the next fifty years the level of carbon dioxide in the atmosphere will be higher than it has been in the last 5 million years — that is well before the period when the ice ages started. Whether this is right or not, it seems unlikely that we can continue to have the luxury of stable sea levels and reliable climates. Agriculture will become progressively more torn between drought and flood, frost and wind, which will make cropping increasingly unreliable, while coastal cities and communities will bear the brunt of tidal surges. Some cities may try to raise funds to build defences, but these may only delay the inevitable process of inundation, which will progressively flood many of the architectural treasures of the world.

The alternative scenario is that the present greenhouse effect may not be enough to counteract the forces leading to the next ice age. It may only temporarily heat the globe until the Earth's orbit goes so deeply into the ice age mode that even the increasing carbon dioxide levels cannot stop the advancing ice. Or, perhaps, the regular sunspot cycle may hesitate again, and hasten the next ice age. Then we could have the luxury of the land surface area increasing again, and be able to find all the archaeological sites around the world that were buried by the Flood. Future archaeologists may even find the stone quarry from which the Devil's Lair chert implements came.

11 Coastal Plain: The Value of Diversity

Heading back towards Perth I stopped at Bunbury to see something quite unexpected so far south. Going along the river bank past a huge mountain of woodchips destined for Japan, I saw open mudflats and then in the distance a grove of dark little trees sprouting from the mud. It reminded me of Singapore where years ago I frequently went into a mangrove swamp near Changi to watch mudskippers, fiddler crabs, and curious jellyfish which lie upside down on the bottom gently pulsating in the sunlight. These jellyfish have algae in their bodies which provide them with all the food they need, as long as they are kept in the sun. Mangroves stretch along most of Australia's northern coasts, providing one of the main nursery grounds for the prawn fishery in Exmouth Gulf. One wonders how long this little patch of mangrove has been growing at Bunbury. It is the most southerly of any found in Western Australia; it could have arrived recently from mangrove seeds which frequently drift down on warm currents from the north, but it is more likely it has been there since the weather was warmer some 6,000 years ago. This was the warmest spell the earth has experienced since long before the last ice age, and could have brought semi-tropical conditions further south.

Following the road up the coast the long line of coastal limestone was visible on the western horizon. This is a tall consolidated sand dune which is due to become a chain of islands if the sea level rises and floods the Leschenault Inlet and Lakes Preston and Clifton. I turned down a side road to Lake Clifton and stopped under some paperbarks to walk to the edge. I went out on to some wet flats with pools of clotted pink "algae". The surface became harder towards the edge of the lake, where waves from the sea breeze were lapping and foaming the dark water against limestone mounds and terraces. The limestone had a familiar form with a layered structure and a characteristic sponginess under the water found in the stromatolites at Shark Bay. Here was another area of living stromatolites, which were not recognised until long after the Shark Bay ones were found.

Stromatolites are commonly found as fossils dating back to the earliest forms of life known some 3,600 million years ago, but few are in existence today. They are built by cyanobacteria, as opposed to the true algae which give the colour to Pink Lake. They are still an important life form, but the conditions which lead them to produce massive structures like stromatolites only rarely occur today. For a long time it was thought that when animals first appeared on Earth, they ate the cyanobacteria and burrowed into stromatolite material so that they could no longer grow into massive structures. But research on the ones at Lake Clifton has shown that this is not the case; it is more probable that conditions leading to their formation are no longer commonly found. One of the important conditions appears to be the flowing of mineral-rich ground-water springs into stable lakes and calm seas subject to evaporation. The coastal plain has huge reserves of ground-water which naturally flow through the limestone and sand towards the sea, coming out as springs along the eastern edge of Lake Clifton. The ground-water responsible for the Hamelin Pool stromatolites originates from artesian water coming from as far away as the Kennedy Ranges; it can be seen flowing from artesian bores in ditches passing under the road near Shark Bay.

I turned over a lump of stromatolite and found it to be crawling with crustaceans; they had bored holes in it but this activity had not stopped it from growing. I went back to the edge of the reeds and sat on a log, watching stilts and other waders feeding along the water's edge. These stromatolites reminded me of the most important innovations which have occurred in living things since the origin of life. These include when the blue-green "algae" first evolved the ability to store the sun's energy by the process of photosynthesis, and when they entered into symbiotic relationships, which led to the origin of plants and animals. These relationships probably also led to the innovation of sexual reproduction, which was maybe the greatest advance of all, because this allowed a complex reassortment of genetic information between individuals and greatly increased the rate of evolution.

This set my mind on to current work on genetic engineering, and what this innovation may have in store for the future of the planet. Up until now, animal and plant species have not been able to exchange genes with one another, except in a few cases, such as between bacteria and closely related species. This is what has ensured the sanctity of species, so that each one can evolve separately with its own gene pool. But it is now possible to add and subtract genes at will, taking genetic material from anywhere in the animal or plant kingdoms. If this could occur naturally, it would be an innovation of similar magnitude to the evolution of sexual reproduction. The fact that it can only occur in the laboratory with specific aims in mind will slow its impact; but we do not know where this activity is going to lead. We are so used to trying to "improve" domestic animals and plants that genetic engineering on these species is bound to become commonplace. Similarly, it will be hard to resist the temptation to remove some genes or add others in the treatment of human disorders, with the aim of improving the quality of life.

The results of these activities will not be without unforeseen problems, which may be like those experienced with the Green Revolution crops. These replaced genetically diverse, well-tried traditional crops, with uniform plants requiring intensive farming techniques. Serious problems have arisen in the form of devastating outbreaks of crop disease, because the new uniform strains lacked resistance. They have also created social problems, because only the rich could afford to grow the new crops. This meant that the poor soon lost their only source of income and this accelerated the movement off the land and into city slums.

Who knows what the ultimate problems will be in tampering with genetic codes. Some find it an exciting goal to give cereal crop plants the ability to produce root nodules like those found in the pea family, and remove the need for nitrogen fertilisers. This would appear to be a thoroughly acceptable aim, although grasses can already fix some nitrogen, but from an ecological point of view this improved ability could mean the final destruction of our remaining natural ecosystems. The new ability may allow the crops, and related weed grasses like wild oats, to invade and exclude all other plants from nutrient-poor natural habitats. Our coastal limestone and jarrah forest may soon look like the African veldt. A similar change took place when the grasses spread in the Miocene as the climate became drier, and caused a major ecological change on the globe, fostering the evolution of huge grazing mammals. These animals, like the giant diprotodons and kangaroos in Australia, ate away the forest boundaries and turned them into grassland. The escape of nodulated grasses and other genetically engineered species into the world's ecosystems could mark mankind's greatest impact on life on Earth.

I was distracted by the sudden arrival of three large march flies (horseflies), which droned around and were dispatched one after the other when they landed on me. This put me in mind of the one-eyed analytical approach which seems to have become ingrained in science. Over the years I have been reading entomological papers on how insects find food sources, such as mosquitoes looking for mammals and blowflies carcasses to lay their eggs in. Research workers use wind tunnels to analyse how insects respond to changes in concentration of smell, treating insects as mindless computers with digital inputs. What has always interested me is why these insects have such noisy wingbeats, especially since it must make them more open to predation. Other similar-sized insects with different food requirements do not have noisy wings, so it would appear that the noise may have a function.

I suspect narrow analytical laboratory studies may miss some of the most important ways in which nature works. With the march flies I have time and again noted how they arrive in pairs or threes, and feel sure that they must cooperate in finding prey, especially as research has shown how difficult it is for a single fly to follow scent up-wind. By using buzzing sounds and watching others, they may be able to follow the other's responses and cooperate in finding the source more rapidly. I'm sure blowflies must

Marchfly or horsefly. Many species are found in Australia and may have long mouthparts to penetrate thick-skinned or furry animals like kangaroos. Most have loud buzzing wingbeats which is possibly a form of communication, but some approach their prey stealthily on soundless wings.

cooperate like this. I remember one occasion when I started frying a steak, and within minutes I heard a strange hum like a swarm of bees coming from down-wind. Within seconds a tight formation of hundreds of blowflies arrived. They must wait around in the bush in prominent positions, like the vultures in Africa, testing the air, watching and listening for others. Of course they may not have well-developed ears like grasshoppers, but they are likely to be sufficiently sensitive to sound. I suspect mosquitoes may cooperate in the same way, because they are very sensitive to sound.

Nature is much more complicated than we can readily appreciate, and as knowledge increases so each scientific discipline becomes progressively more narrow and finely analytical, many trying to emulate the physical sciences. This thought makes me particularly worried about any assertions about the harmless nature of subjects chosen for genetic engineering. Many who make these assertions are unlikely to have the experience to appreciate the wider complexities of nature or to synthesise the global body of scientific knowledge. Synthesis on this scale tends not to be regarded as "science" and is usually omitted from university curricula. The present climate of scientific funding does not help, with flavour-of-the-month, goal-oriented research tending to be backed at the expense of fundamental research. One can imagine huge sums of money being put into research with the aim of producing an engineered crop that can be patented and sold for profit, but which lacks the necessary thought and rigorous analysis on possible side-effects. On the other hand, one can expect little funding to be available for work on how ecosystems function, even though this knowledge is vital in order to manage the world environment as well as to identify the likely damaging effects of each innovation *before* it is released into the environment.

There is no doubt that genetic engineering is here to stay and will make profound changes in the world, but, like nuclear science, Green Revolution plants and organochlorine pesticides, many of the resulting problems will be unforeseen and come with potentially devastating consequences. Particularly worrying is the trend for products which are banned in their country of origin being sold in countries which lack appropriate legislation or control. One can foresee experimental work which is banned in one country being funded in another for the profit motive, or undertaken in defence departments which, by their nature, lack scrutiny and normal ethical controls. (The incredible contamination problems caused by lack of control on nuclear weapons plants in America are well-known and I can remember the day when my father, as a parasitologist, was taken on a tour of the highly secret biological warfare establishment in England at a time when the country was supposedly not involved in such work.)

I travelled north towards Mandurah, arriving at one of the new canal developments where I joined a group of friends on a houseboat to go down Western Australia's Murray River. The land is very low-lying and the river meanders through she-oak-covered banks into a delta running into the Peel/Harvey Estuary. There were a remarkable number of birds along the river, especially darters and cormorants indicating an abundance of fish. We also saw herons, spoonbill, black ducks, wood ducks, black swans, rails, moorhens and coots, as well as a large flotilla of pelicans, as we entered the estuary. This is a wonderful nursery for marine life, which has made it one of the most important recreation areas around Perth, for fishing, boating and crabbing.

In recent years changes have made the area become less attractive. The waters turn brown in summer and a bluish bloom sweeps in towards the shore, depositing a thick, stinking sludge. This is mainly made up of the blue-green "alga" *Nodularia* which grows like a poisonous disease in waters rich in phosphorus and nitrogen. To people living nearby the smell must be reminiscent of the canals of Bangkok or Venice. Extensive works have been conducted to try and alleviate the problem, especially by increasing the flushing rate and deepening the ocean channel; there are also plans for digging a new one. Some enterprising people have even benefited from the sludge, turning it into a fertiliser business; a pioneer mass bacterial harvesting program.

The most productive approach to the problem has been to identify and address the cause, which was found to be fertilisers getting into the ground water and seeping into the river and estuary. Most farmers are now cooperating by cutting their fertiliser applications to such a level that little gets as far as the ground water. However, other problem industries are emerging, such as pig-farming activities. It is hoped that in the course of time more of the area will be given over to people and recreation interests, while rural industries will be encouraged to leave the coastal plain. Eventually much of the area should be covered by forestry operations which would restore the health of the estuary, although great changes are likely if the sea level rises. Then one may see Thames-like barriers being placed at the river mouth.

No doubt the same pollution problems may come to Lake Clifton, with the springs becoming contaminated with nutrients, and the *Nodularia* sludge replacing the stromatolite-forming bacteria. Eventually the whole area is likely to be swamped by higher water tables, in which case the winners may be the birds, which will have their area of coastal swamp and marshland greatly extended.

Huge tangles of spiders' web made it difficult to walk through the reeds and paperbarks near the entrance of the Serpentine River. Most were made

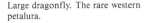

Large dragonfly. The rare western petalura.

Christmas Spider, a social species building communal webs. Spines may be to discourage birds from eating them.

by Christmas spiders which are a highly social species, cooperating in building their complex, tangled webs. The spiders have spines on their bodies to dissuade predators if the sticky web is not enough in itself. Higher up, strung between the trees, there were some huge webs spun by golden-orb spiders. These are a tropical group of spiders which often build their webs amongst telephone wires in places like Bali, and use a gold-coloured silk. The huge female builds a double web with a line of debris in it to warn birds against flying through it. Looking carefully at one web I could see tiny silver blobs moving on the strands, which turned out to be a parasitic spider. This species only lives in other spiders' webs. There were also a number of small male golden-orbs, which also live like parasites in the female's web.

One web had caught a huge dragonfly, rather similar to one I knew from England. I have long had an interest in dragonflies, having graduated from flies, which I found were too difficult to identify. Dragonflies are remarkable insects and were the first large flying predator to evolve on Earth. They grew to an enormous size in the Carboniferous, but lost their supremacy when the pterosaurs evolved; these dinosaurs were apparently covered in fur and were probably rather like diurnal bats. It is interesting that dragonflies have been able to preserve their niche, even in the face of competition and predation by pterosaurs and birds.

Dragonflies have their uses today, because they can indicate the state of fresh-water bodies. People love to live near lakes and rivers, but by living near them they change the nature of the water, causing escalating management problems and the need to control water quality. One problem comes from mosquitoes, which are particularly bad after floods and high tides in late spring. These may lead to public health concerns such as the appearance of Ross River virus, which erupts periodically. Malaria is another problem which could emerge, because the disease is being brought in at an increasing rate by overseas travellers. Malaria used to be endemic in Britain, and could become so here, although the local mosquitoes are not efficient carriers of the disease. (The mosquitoes that cause most problems in the Perth area do not breed in lakes at all, but in puddles in watered gardens, septic tanks, water-filled gutters and potted plants, so it is important to identify the species before blaming the lakes.)

For most of the year mosquito numbers are kept low in lakes by an abundance of predators which eat the larvae, especially dragonfly nymphs, beetles and water-boatmen. However, the lakes change as urban development grows: the fringe of vegetation declines, the number of birds increases, exotic fish become established, and fertilisers flow into the lake from the ground water. The changes create an unstable environment, where algal blooms can grow on the fertilisers and bird droppings, and where insect predators are eaten by fish and birds. This leads to a much more simplified ecology, where an algal sludge predominates and acts as a predator-free culture-medium for midges. These insects are not a biting species, but have an incredible nuisance value, with millions swarming to lights at night. They are somewhat mosquito-like in appearance, so there is an erroneous tendency to label them as a "mosquito problem".

Healthy lakes may have more than six species of dragonfly living in them, but the worst affected, like Lake Monger, have none. This is partly because councils resort to using insecticides when the midge problem gets serious. This is the final straw in the process of degradation, which sees large numbers of birds dying in summer, when the algal sludge becomes infected with botulism and occasionally laced with insecticide. Several other remedies are possible; the most sensible for new lakes is not to site houses too close and to ensure that there is a good barrier of trees around the edge to hold the midges. Deepening the lakes and trying to cut the amount of fertiliser used in the area may also help. Another idea I have floated is to try to divert midges from household lights by putting bright lights near the lake.

It is amazing how noisy midges can be. Walking along the edge of Lake Forrestdale my feet disturbed midges resting in the grass and brought about an incredible whine around my ankles. I remember one evening hearing a large swarm of midges developing in the warm air rising above the van. It was a while before I could see them, because they were so small and darting so rapidly, but the noise grew in intensity until the swarm emerged like a column of smoke. Midges and mosquitoes have a well-developed sense of hearing, using an organ at the base of their feathery antennae. I found that any sound I made sent the swarm into a frenzied burst of whining activity, condensing out of the air and diffusing again. The purpose of the

Black-winged stilt *(below)*: a widespread species found around lakes and rivers. The local banded stilt is restricted to Australia, and is found in huge flocks on Rottnest Island during the summer.

Darter, a relative of cormorants and pelicans. These birds swim with only the head and neck above water making them look like a snake swimming, and are sometimes known as snake-birds.

Living stromatolites. These limestone structures are built by cyanobacteria. They are mainly found as fossils dating back to the earliest appearance of life on Earth. Living are comparatively rare now, with the best known being found at Shark Bay. These ones are growing on the shore of Lake Clifton near Mandurah.

Bog-loving dragonfly. This tiny species *(Nannophya dalei)* breeds in similar places to the giant western petalura. It is found flying around permanent, spring-fed bogs and swamps.

Coastal swampland. Most permanent swamps and bogs are now so altered by agriculture, grazing stock, or introduced weeds like these calla lilies, that the rare western petalura dragonfly can no longer breed there.

Blackboys in the hills. Following streams into the hills one passes scenes such as this. It demonstrates the process of change which is affecting all native vegetation and wildlife habitats. These blackboys are all that remains of a complex vegetation. Frequent fires and drifting grass seed mean that all the native vegetation will eventually be replaced by exotic grasses, even in forested areas. This process will be greatly speeded up if genetic engineers manage to get cereal grasses to form root nodules like plants in the pea family.

whining sound is to enable them to form swarms and to attract females from a great distance. The females fly into the swarm and fall out mating with a successful male.

Over the years I have followed my interest in dragonflies, and on arriving in Australia my attention was naturally drawn to a particularly large species which had been collected near Perth in the 1950s. It was an unusual one also because, unlike nearly all others, its nymphs feed out of water, crawling around over wet mud and only retreating to holes in the swamp during daylight hours. Its habitat was supposed to be "permanent, spring-fed swamps" — quite a rare habitat in dry Western Australia. Over many years I searched for this species without any success; most of these habitats had been turned into farm dams, were grazed and trampled by cattle or, like Bull Creek, were now built-up areas. However, I found some wonderful dragonfly places, like Bennet and Gingin Brooks, which were like tropical water gardens with the air full of dragonflies. But still there was no sign of the species I was looking for. Eventually I decided to spend a week looking for it in all likely places between Perth and Lake Muir near Manjimup.

After a long search I eventually found some living beside a forest stream above the Logue Brook Dam. It was a great lumbering species with rather odd behaviour patterns; for instance, it rested near the bases of young trees, on the trunk where it looked rather like a projecting twig. It was also difficult to disturb, as if it did not like flying in the daytime, so I wondered if it may only fly at dusk like several other dragonflies. I was relieved that the species was still in existence, but it must be under great threat of extinction, because of its restricted habitat and long life history.

I began to think about the reasons for preserving rare species. It has always posed a problem for me when trying to explain the reasons to environmental philistines. One is soon backed into a corner clutching at straws, such as: "So that scientists can study them", "They are a legacy which we should not destroy", or "They are beautiful and enhance the countryside". More recently reasons have included "They may be useful", and "They are part of the world ecology on which we depend for our existence".

Trying to look into the future gives a glimpse of how important it may really be to maintain species diversity. Scientists are becoming increasingly worried over factors such as the Green Revolution, which is sweeping away genetic diversity in crops, or marketing trends which are similarly removing thousands of local varieties. One only needs to look at the apples of Europe — they have changed from an enormous variety, to a few plastic-looking, unvarying products. Plant breeders well know the need for maintaining genetic diversity, especially when new strains of pest or disease appear. Genes in wild relatives have already proved to be invaluable in keeping domestic varieties healthy. Even so, the remaining stocks of local varieties of vegetables which have been kept in a few government research centres in Britain are soon likely to be lost in a cost-cutting exercise. Hope comes from a plan to lay down seed banks in mines cut in the tundra permafrost.

This does not help species like my dragonflies. Perhaps it could be argued that they could be "useful" in other ways, such as controlling waterborne pests, but this is unlikely. The real answer may lie in the more distant future. We are just embarking on a new phase in our evolution — the "Post-Neolithic" as I call it — when our intelligence begins to crawl out of its Stone-Age swamp. Our science is telling us something about the life around us, which does make it very important indeed. For a start it is obvious to anyone that living things are incredible; just try making a microchip-powered model of a midge, or even a dragonfly on the same scale, and you will see what I mean! High technology, aeons beyond our own power, has evolved by the slow process of natural selection and has resulted, after 4,000 million years, in the animals and plants we see today.

We treat these animals and plants as the ignorant Vandals treated the bastions of Roman culture. However, we now know that within each species there is a library which can create a living thing, its complex structure, sense organs, behaviour and physiology. We cannot read it yet, but we are beginning to find some of the key words and are rapidly applying them through genetic engineering. Cellulose fibres are being made using bacteria and this development could make paper-making from timber obsolete. Now we find that the groundwork has been done to start making textiles from spiders' web, using the relevant spider gene implanted into bacteria, and insect sense organs are being used as the most sensitive chemical detection system yet available. It is an exciting time. Soon we may see keratin fibres being produced using merino genes, marking the demise of sheep farming, and animal proteins being grown in bacterial culture to make the meat industry obsolete. It all rests on the move to a form of factory farming based on algae as the primary producers.

The combined genetic pool of the world's species gives future generations an immense library from which recipes can be drawn for making unbelievable human-fostered technologies. Vandalising it now will mean the Earth has to wait another 40 million years for it to regain its complexity. Fortunately for each species lost, in the same way as with vandalised libraries, not all the information is lost, because others may hold many of the lost volumes. Some are unique to a species, including its unique assemblage of genetic information, but it may be possible to almost rebuild its genetic structure from related species. Ninety-eight per cent of our genetic information could be reconstructed from chimpanzees, and probably more if orang-utans and gorillas were included. However, we tend to think that the missing bits may be the most important! I was reminded of the little spider found in Kings Park and now extinct — could it have had a gene which gave its silk a special quality that would have been as useful in silk-biotechnology as that which gives merino wool its quality? Future textile technologists will not have the option of finding out.

What, then, is likely to be useful in this huge dragonfly? Nobody knows, but one is led to ask, does it *have to be useful* to be worth keeping? Maybe just because it exists is enough to make it important; it represents an incredible technology, brought about by millions of years of natural processes, and is part of the world ecosystem. Is that not enough? Libraries are not only there for us to use for reference purposes; they are also for us to enjoy reading for pleasure alone. Some people even keep books purely for their aesthetic value.

Kestrels hover in the wind by rapidly beating their wings and twisting their tails so that their heads and eyes remain virtually motionless in relation to the ground. This allows them to see small movements in the grass made by lizards and insects.

12 Rottnest: Ecology and Human Society

Setting off for Rottnest Island always instils a feeling of separation or finality, like going for an overseas holiday, even though it is only an hour away from Fremantle by boat. The car is left behind, as is the telephone and all the commitments of the mainland. The crossing even has some of the characteristics of a sea voyage, with a stretch of ocean swell which regularly quells high-spirited day-trippers. While looking out over the cobalt blue waters and watching small powerboats tumbling in the sea I usually catch a glimpse of a flying fish speeding away from the bow-wave. It reminds me of crossing the Atlantic on a small cargo boat heading for Trinidad and of how the ocean changed colour as the days progressed, from the dark ultramarine hues of the plankton-rich North Atlantic to the relatively plankton-free cobalt blue of the tropics. Swarms of flying fish sped away from the bows of the boat, together with groups of flying squid. The latter pink animals are almost as good at flying, although they cannot power themselves for a further flight like the fish. I have watched some fish dip their elongated tailfins in the waves several times, and re-enter the water some 300 metres away. There were also many dolphins which gambolled in the bow-wave, often getting excited and darting off to play, leaping high out of the water and crashing into the waves.

One can often see dolphins on the way to Rottnest, and sometimes whales and sea lions. It is remarkable to think that scientists once said that it was physically impossible for dolphins to go as fast as the boats they were obviously lapping. Research eventually discovered that they had a specially adapted skin which allowed them to go so fast, and the findings are now applied to submarines. Much of our technology could have been invented earlier had we looked at how animals and plants do things first; it is all part of the vast biological "library" available for those who can read it.

Approaching the Caribbean the waters turned a murky green with the vast quantities of fresh water flowing in from the Amazon, Orinoco and many other rivers draining the South American rainforest. Some, like the Demerara River, were already heavily silt-laden from bauxite mining and logging activities. The colour of the water on approaching Rottnest has none of this. It still has a brilliant, almost fluorescent turquoise quality, reminiscent of tropical coral reefs. The colour is found in places with clear

Avocets—a common sight around the salt lakes at Rottnest.

blue skies, clear plankton-free shallow water, a clean white shell-sand bottom, and is best when the sun is high.

I left the boat at Thompson Bay and took a bicycle through the Settlement, past Garden Lake to the Causeway between Government House and Herschel Lakes. Flocks of small birds were busy at the waterside, feeding along the edge on a pink sludge. They included some ruddy turnstones, red-necked stints, a few banded stilts and a pair of avocets. Across the lake there were some large shimmering "islands" entirely made up of banded stilts.

These lakes are now particularly rich in food for birds, because they have enormous populations of brine shrimps which get washed up along the lea shores. These shrimps are not native to Australia, and probably became established in the lake when saltwork machinery was brought to the island many years ago. This machinery was probably contaminated with eggs when it was imported from another part of the globe. The saltworks has gone now, but not the brine shrimp which thrives on the pink algae and bacteria inhabiting the salt lakes.

The banded stilts make Rottnest their summer home, spreading out over mainland salt lakes during the winter, where they breed in good years. Many of the other birds come from much further afield, like the red-necked stints, ruddy turnstones, grey-tailed tattlers and sanderlings, which breed in areas near the Arctic, especially Siberia and Alaska, and migrate here for the northern winter.

Further along I noticed some little birds drinking near the water's edge. They were a pair of white-fronted chats. These birds, like the crimson chats I saw at Eyre, have a remarkable ability to detect salt, and will not touch water with salt levels much lower than that we can taste. It was strange for these birds to be drinking at the edge of the salt lake, where salt levels are much higher than sea water. However, a close look at the water they were drinking showed it to be full of detritus, mosquito larvae and covered in swarms of a swampfly. It was not in fact lake water, but a fresh water spring flowing out of the limestone. These springs extend around the lakes in patches, coming from lenses of fresh water in the limestone. The water comes from rain falling on the limestone hills and soaking through to the salt watertable. Quokkas regularly drink from these springs and foul them with their droppings.

The water probably contains much dissolved lime, because it runs through a labyrinth of water-filled caverns cut out of the limestone. In fact the lakes are thought to have been formed when cavern systems collapsed in the past. The fresh water is now being pumped out to supply the Settlement, hopefully not lowering the watertable far enough to deprive the chats of their water supply. Other springs are salt water, such as along the northern shore of Lake Bagdad, where sea water enters the lake system. Crabs and other marine life can be found living there.

At the end of the Causeway I could see where the saltworks had stood, and on the other side of the road a kestrel hovered over a limestone hill, looking for lizards and grasshoppers almost as if it were a kite held there by an unseen wire. Kestrels are one of the few birds of prey which have avoided pesticide poisoning in England. This is because they tend to feed on lizards and insects instead of the pesticide-containing birds which most raptors feed on.

Seeing these birds always reminds me of how language evolves with time, because their old name, *windfucker*, is a graphic example. The name described the quivering wing movements while hovering, but when the word acquired its modern usage, polite society had to find an alternative name for the bird. "Windhover" was tried, but "casterel" derived from the bird's call was already in use, and the modern form of this name is now dominant. Words and pronunciation continue to evolve at a great rate in our society, much to the annoyance of the older generation, but spelling tends to be fossilised by dictionaries and the education system, which demand conformity with past ideals.

Science is one of the most prolific areas for spawning new words, which are often frighteningly complex. They are used as a form of shorthand for scientists to communicate with one another, but they have the effect of turning many people away from the subject. Scientific language has another unfortunate use in social contexts, when scientists will use their Latinised jargon to put lay-people in their place. In fact the use of Latin possibly has its origin in this function, replacing Druid jargon or "mumbo-jumbo" with another form of mumbo-jumbo, which had the effect of ensuring that the common people remained lay-people. The educated elite also began to use Latin as a form of code to keep their ideas from the masses, but eventually education brought Latin to the general population and it lost its point; its use has declined and even the Latin Mass has gone. Scientists still cling to their jargon, often feeling incredibly insecure when trying to use common language to describe their work. Some may even unconsciously use a different pronunciation of a Latin word to undermine the status of a knowledgeable lay-person. Perhaps this merely demonstrates that scientists are no different from anyone else in human society, because language is universally used to identify positions in the social heirarchy as well as to communicate.

My eyes fell on the tangled vegetation below the kestrel and the grey scalloped limestone structure of the hill. Looking along the hill I could see parallel indentations cut into the rock at various levels, with the most obvious at the base. This undercut is exactly like the one found around the present shores of the island, where the sea comes over a flat platform or reef and crashes against a limestone cliff. The cut around the lakes clearly indicates where the sea level was some time ago, when breakers swelled into the area. Detailed studies of these cuts provide us with a picture of recent sea level changes; a careful look at the rock face shows that the rock indentations have encrusting shells of serpulid worms which live below the sea, so it is thought that the lower cuts were formed before the uppermost. Some of the cuts are so small that the sea level can only have been stationary for a few hundred years. The highest cut is 2.6 metres above the present sea level, and has been dated at about 5,000 years ago. This is the time when the Earth's climate was at its warmest, and civilisation was booming in the lush pastures of the now arid Middle East. After this notch was formed, something dramatic took place, because the sea level suddenly changed without leaving any notches. Evidence elsewhere shows that the sea level did fall, before stabilising at the present level, but the sudden move at Rottnest suggests that there may have been a movement along the Darling Fault, possibly a huge earthquake, which raised Rottnest to its present height above sea level.

Below the present sea level, there is an undercut around the island, which is a favourite hiding spot for rock lobsters, and there must be many more notches out to sea, with perhaps a large one around the Swan Canyon and along the continental shelf fourteen kilometres west of Rottnest. This would have formed when the sea level was 130 metres below the present level, 18,000 years ago. The present reefs and notch appear to be unique, because the sea level has been ever-changing in the past, with only brief stops, yet for the last 5,000 years it has been virtually stationary, producing extensive reef platforms.

I looked more closely at the limestone and found it to be full of fossils. Most of the coastal limestone is made from consolidated shell-sand dunes, but these rocks included coral reefs. This is only to be expected as the sea level was so much higher in the past, but the kinds of coral are rather different from those growing here now. They include the warm-water staghorn corals, which are now only found as far south as the Abrolhos Islands near Geraldton. Dating these fossils has shown them to be about 100,000 years old, indicating that the sea level was again high, during the last interglacial period, and that the climate was even warmer than at its recent peak 5,000 years ago. I wondered how long it will be before the sea breaks into the lakes again. Probably not in my lifetime, but even with the most optimistic projections of the greenhouse effect, rising sea levels may soon send breakers crashing into the Rottnest shore well above the worst known storms in history.

A quokka hopped out from the undercut and went down to the edge of the lake, reminding me of the biological effects of sea-level changes. Eighteen thousand years ago Rottnest would have been a conspicuous hill sticking out of the huge coastal plain area. It would have been covered by tuart forest and swamps, and occupied by a wide range of wildlife hunted by the local people. As the flood commenced, everything would have been pushed back before the encroaching sea until Rottnest became a peninsula joined to the mainland through Carnac and Garden Islands, about 7,000 years ago. So in only 500 years the island was cut off, with whatever animals and plants were living on it at that time. There were probably kangaroos, various wallabies, thylacines, marsupial mice and various rodents. Over the years since it was cut off, the flora and fauna evolved like those on the Recherche Archipelago, with various species dying out and a few arriving to replace them. Large predators would have been some of the first to die out because such a small island could only support a very small population. These would quickly become inbred and lose their genetic diversity, making them more prone to the forces leading to extinction.

The lottery of survival has led to only one mammal and one predatory snake surviving on each of Rottnest and Garden Islands. Rottnest has the quokka and dugite, Garden Island the tammar wallaby and tiger snake. Carnac was too small for wallabies to survive, but has lots of tiger snakes. The original tuart forest died out with the exposure to high winds and salt-spray, and was replaced by coastal species, especially the Rottnest Island pine, Rottnest tea tree and the coastal wattle *Acacia rostellifera*.

It is somewhat odd to find the quokka on Rottnest, because surveys on the mainland have shown that this animal is a swamp-living species, still common in many south-west forest and coastal swamps. Yet on Rottnest it lives all over the island, often in very arid conditions with hardly any swamps. It is possible that the salt lakes were once extensive freshwater swamps supporting a large quokka population before the island was cut off from the mainland. They may have only slowly become salt after the island was formed, and as other species died out and the predators disappeared, the quokka progressively found it was free to exploit the whole island. This gives a glimpse into some of the intricacies of natural ecology.

Much descriptive work on animals and plants relates to how they are adapted to living in their natural environments; how they cope with stress from lack of water, high temperatures, poor foods and so on. Yet sometimes, as with the quokkas, their distribution has nothing to do with these adaptations. A clue as to why this is so comes from the woylies, which are basically a desert-adapted species, yet have only survived in the forest. This is because the forest was the only place where they could escape fox predation, even though the cool damp conditions in the south-west do not suit them as well. Quokkas may be the same, only living in swamps and having become adapted to living in them because that is where they can escape large predators such as the thylacine. On Rottnest there are no predators or competitors so they are free to go wherever they can survive, which is virtually everywhere.

Human populations resemble the quokkas, having lost previous external

Salmon Point, Rottnest Island. The island is surrounded by a flat limestone reef which has been formed out of the ancient sand-dunes which make up the island. The reef demonstrates that the sea-level has changed very little in the last 6000 years, but other reefs and notches in the limestone show that the sea-level has been much less stable in the past.

Rottnest Island from the air. Shows the salt lakes, which are thought to have been formed by the collapse of limestone caverns. The island vegetation used to be made up mainly of a cover of trees and shrubs, but fire and quokka grazing have removed most of this, replacing them with a tough, sharp-leaved lily.

Mountain ducks. These attractive birds inhabit the salt lakes. They are a kind of shelduck, most species of which are very colourful and adapted to living in marine areas and saltmarshes. They feed by paddling their feet in the mud to stir up the bottom, as shown, then filtering off the disturbed food.

Quokka. These small wallabies occur in great numbers on Rottnest Island. Their rat-like tails led Vlamingh to give the island its name. There are no large predators on the island, so the animals have no fear, and do not have normal controls on their numbers. In the 6000 years since the island was cut off from the mainland they have changed from the mainland form, which is larger and more aggressive towards other members of its own species.

Fish Hook Bay. This attractive bay on the west end of Rottnest is inhabited by a number of tropical species of marine life. Warm sea currents bring tropical water onto the south and western shores of the island and encourage the growth of corals and a rich variety of reef fish. The north and east shores have cooler waters in winter, so are mainly populated by species preferring the temperate southern coast of Australia.

Radiata pine on Rottnest. Various attempts have been made to replace the original tree-cover of the island, which had been lost by fires and quokka grazing. There are a number of plantations, protected by wire fences including some of pine. The salt-laden air soon rots the wire and the quokkas get in. When hard-pressed for food they will even climb trees to feed: they have climbed this wire to feed on pine bark.

Ospreys at their nest. There are a number of osprey nests around the edge of the island. They mainly choose isolated rocky stacks surrounded by water, but some are connected to the land at low tide. They catch fish in their talons and carry them with the head into the wind to reduce air resistance.

controls so that they are spreading throughout the island-like planet, and even occupying its seas and frozen wastes. The social relationships of quokkas also show similarities with human society. The mainland quokkas are like many other animals which are aggressive towards others. This has the effect of pushing excess young and subordinate animals into the fringes of the best habitat, where they are quickly taken by predators. This activity makes sure that the populations never become dense enough to graze away the vegetation to such an extent that thylacines or foxes can come in and kill them. On Rottnest, however, predation and cover are no longer so important, and the animals have changed their behaviour patterns and become much more tolerant of others. They build up into dense aggregations and eat the vegetation away, destroying their habitat much like human societies are doing. They have even lost most of their ability to escape predators, so they would have little chance of survival if returned to the mainland. Attempts have been made to establish them on a fenced reserve near Perth, but few have survived, even under expensive protection. Many fell to foxes which can climb the fences, and others may have died from lack of resistance to some mainland viral diseases no longer present on the island.

I got back on to my bicycle and headed for West End to get there before the sea breeze arrived. I can sit there for hours watching the scene near Cape Vlamingh, with its roaring breakers crashing over the reefs, the boobies and terns diving into the sea, the dolphins surfing on the breakers or whales spouting near the horizon. Nearby, there were parties of crested turns resting on the limestone headlands, crabs clambering over the rockface or scurrying away from an octopus, and fish swimming over the beds of sea-urchins on the reef platform.

The marine life on Rottnest is particularly interesting because it is where temperate and tropical species meet. The onshore current on the south and west of the island is warm, so the animals that live there are mainly tropical species. They include many corals, and their associated fauna which is quite as rich as that found in the tropics, and ninety species of tropical fish. The east and north of the island tend to have cooler waters in winter and this is where a southern temperate fauna predominates.

Looking at the notch cut by 5,000 years of wave-action, I could see many limpets and winkle shells. This rock is pounded by severe waves, yet is the home of many animals which have evolved ways of firmly sticking themselves down. This habitat has an abundant food supply coming from algae growing on the rock, while for much of the time the shells are out of reach of predators, such as the octopi and starfish. However, a whelk shell has become adapted to this habitat and preys on the limpets, drilling holes in their shells and sucking the animal out. The whelk is clever in this Dracula-like activity, because it avoids damaging the limpet's muscles and the shell remains stuck to the rock while the whelk performs its deadly deed.

It is interesting to see how the winkles differ in their adaptations. High

A shell commonly washed up on Australian coasts. It belongs to a deep sea relative of the squids and fossil ammonites. The shell is grown inside the animal, and is used as a float like a fish's swim bladder. The shell floats to the surface when the animal dies, and is blown on-shore.

up on the rocks in the area splashed by winter storms, dozens of little white or grey winkles cluster in hollows to avoid the drying summer sun. Below them are the greenish-white species, which get wet each time the tide comes in. Then at the base there is a black one with a thick shell to protect it from predators while under the water. It is a fairly simple ecological system where one can test ideas on distributions and populations. Does the presence of one species influence the distribution of another? Does the density of a population determine how far it spreads up the rockface? Are there genetic differences within a species which allow it to occupy different habitats? Does food influence density?

Many experiments have been carried out on these lines and the answers are mainly: yes. One of the earliest experiments resolved a problem with the two sorts of rock crabs. Statistical studies clearly showed that the purple form lived higher up the rockface than the orange ones, but because their anatomies were virtually identical (museum specimens lost their distinctive colours anyway) taxonomists regarded them as belonging to the same species. However, a study involving a form of genetic fingerprinting showed that there was no gene transfer between the two colour forms and no hybrids, so the two forms were indeed two separate species. Many other species do not have the advantage of colour differences for us to see, so go undetected until geneticists have reason to study them. This is mainly done with pests for economic purposes, in a similar way to genetic fingerprinting on people being usually only done for legal purposes. It has recently been found that the pest of jarrah trees, the jarrah leaf miner, is not the same species as the leaf miner which defoliates flooded gums on the coastal plain. If studies such as this could be extended to the bulk of species on earth, then we would find that there are very many more than we suspect.

I was curious about some behaviour patterns of the winkles. How do they know when they have got to the right height above the waves? What happens when they get knocked off and have to find their way back? I tried putting a handful of shells on a rock at the base of the notch and watched to see what happened, using time-lapse photography to record everything. The film showed the clump springing to life with the pile of shells pulsating and revolving for quite a while until, suddenly, one took off and the whole pile immediately followed in single file like a chain of beads. The snails must use their slime-trails as a form of communication, possibly marking the zone they inhabit so that they know where they are.

I watched mirages approaching over the sea, with waves reflected in the sky above the horizon. This meant that the sea breeze was on its way in and it would soon be too cool and windy to stay, so I cycled along the road back towards the Settlement. Many of the trees at the roadside had wire-netting around the base to stop quokkas attacking them. The area inside the wire was thick with vegetation compared with outside, but some quokkas had actually climbed the trees and ringbarked the branches, especially in one "radiata" pine-plantation. Some of the trees planted were tuarts, which looked very sick because they are not able to cope with the wind and salt spray. Later plantings included more tea trees because they are better adapted to growing along the coast.

It is interesting to see what has happened in this simple island ecology, where there is an uncontrolled population of quokkas and a limited vegetation. When the first Europeans saw the island, they mainly saw a dense thicket of tea trees and Rottnest Island pines. This was partly because they landed in the Thompson Bay area and did not struggle through the thicket to see the rest of the island. Towards the west they would have seen open hills and dense aca⁻ia thickets as well as more pines and tea trees. The quokka population as high then, but the dense canopy probably prevented as much ground vegetation growing as there is now, so the quokkas had less food and the population was smaller. Clearing and burning changed all that. It brought all vegetation down to the level of the quokka so that the population boomed and they grazed everything, including any regenerating trees. The result has been that the island has become covered in the vegetation which the quokka likes grazing least, which is a sharp ankle-binding plant in the lily family (*Acanthocarpus*) and some introduced plants including stinging nettles and onion weed. Active management is underway to try to restore some of the thicket areas and control quokka access in the hope that the population may become more stable.

I went down to the shore at City of York Bay and sat on the beach. The shell-sand included the disc-like skeletons of a single-celled foraminiferan and the delicate spiral shells from a deep-sea, nautilus-like animal (*Spirula*). This animal uses its shell as a float so that it can stay mid-water without swimming, like the ammonites used to do millions of years ago. I watched an osprey fly past clutching a fish, perhaps it was carrying it to its young in the nest on Crayfish Rock. I began to think about the quokkas and how similar their plight is to our own. Their normal forms of mortality have gone, as there are no predators to kill excess young, yet the island can support only a finite number of animals. Something has to give, so far it is only the vegetation. Predation as a means of controlling human populations disappeared some time ago, but disease and tribal strife took over. Now we are doing everything in our power to remove disease, improve nutrition, and stop head-hunting, and we wonder why we have a world population problem! We are at about the stage of the quokka after the 1955 fire which opened a huge area of the island to more intensive grazing.

The quokkas at the moment have a rough existence, experiencing much stress during winter because of the cold, lack of shelter and excessive water in their diet. The young are in the pouch all this time, first coming out in spring. The food improves and it becomes warmer so that everything looks fine, but as summer wears on, pressures work to a head because the population is too dense and something has to give. Larger animals chase smaller ones out of the better areas. The smaller ones move into less good habitat and lose condition, eating what is left of the vegetation, getting sick and eventually dying of causes brought on by partial starvation. On the mainland they would have been picked off by predators long before this time, saving the vegetation from such excessive grazing pressure.

The situation is made worse by the Settlement and rubbish tips, because here the quokkas can obtain high quality food during the summer, and so have better survival chances and more successful breeding. This tends to be reflected in the poorer areas which are put under greater stress from these animals. The worst fate for the island quokka population would be if one summer it rained enough to enable most of the animals to survive. The resulting population boom could well lead to a speedy extinction. The result would be like unthinkingly giving food-aid to famine-stricken peoples where the extra food ensures that the next famine will come sooner and will cause greater suffering and environmental destruction.

A strange consequence of the dense quokka population is that they have become largely immune to local diseases. The island would naturally have had salmonella food-poisoning organisms, which are particularly common in reptiles, but the density of the quokka populations has greatly boosted the infection rate. In summer virtually 100 per cent of quokkas have food-poisoning organisms in their stomachs and intestines, often with several forms at once. The quokkas seem to be largely unaffected by the thirty-four kinds known on the island and are even immune to the effects of the many new forms of food-poisoning which have been brought in by visitors. This immunity is perhaps detrimental to the population because a greater disease-induced mortality-rate would relieve the stress on the island and lead to a healthier residual population. However, the isolation of the quokkas on the island means they have probably lost immunity to many other common organisms, and could be decimated by a disease brought from the mainland, in the same way that the Aborigines were killed by many European diseases.

We now know that the world human population is on an island in space and that there is a very definite limit to growth. Attempts are being made to limit human population growth, but it will be a long time before we can expect even the most drastic population control programs to bring about a reversal. The world population may well have quadrupled before any real control is developed unless, of course, something like the quokka summer-drought controls us, or AIDS comes to the rescue of the planet.

It is interesting that most attempts to alleviate the problems experienced by disadvantaged peoples appear to backfire, such as giving food-aid, missions, medicine, Green-Revolution crops, arms intervention, international loans, even "equality". The introduction of the "Post-Neolithic" microbe-based economies could be seen as a godsend to the globe, defusing our interventionist way of life and taking the main pressures of material, food and energy production off the most vegetated parts of the world and relocating them in more arid areas. This technology may be mainly for the developed world, so there are bound to be unfortunate results which could further disadvantage the developing countries which do not have the financial resources to use this technology. Ideally the industry should be developed on a global scale, ignoring international boundaries. There is also the risk that the new technology could produce enough food and materials to encourage the world population to go on increasing, which would definitely lead to inevitable disaster.

Back on the jetty I looked into the water and saw a jellyfish gently pulsating in the water, apparently aimlessly drifting by. We look on the jellyfish as a primitive form of life, but in its day this was the ultimate level of high technology. These animals had evolved over a very long period of time from single cells sticking together and "learning" to cooperate with one another until, finally, the jellyfish structure was born out of an enormous "society" of cells. This jellyfish may appear simple, but it represents one of the greatest breakthroughs during the evolution of life. It is a massive organism made up of millions of individual cells, placed exactly where they should be and working in a remarkably coordinated way to produce a very functional whole.

I began to wonder about human society. Are we the cells in a new level of complexity? There can be little doubt about that, but we have a long way to go until we reach the stage of the jellyfish. Wasps and ants are way ahead of us in terms of organisation and genetic programming, as they can produce castes and clones to do particular jobs. We have the advantage of being able to bypass their snail-pace process of genetic evolution, because our society could be changed by a conscious process if only we knew how to do it. We may soon even have the ability to produce human clones and castes at will, abhorrent though it may seem, through genetic engineering and IVF programs. However, we still do not know where we are going, and our society still flounders around like a proto-jellyfish, disintegrating as fast as we put bits together. In fact it seems that the longer we hold bits together the deeper the cancers become, and the more devastating the chaos which ensues. The risks of superpower conflict seem to be abating, but this is having the effect of lifting the lid on internal conflicts, and between smaller nations which appear just as frightening. No doubt there is some super-intelligence out there watching in a bemused fashion as we flounder around unable to build ourselves into jellyfish, let alone drag ourselves out of the swamp.

I wonder when the "Post-Neolithic" will begin? It needs massive capital, so in purely commercial terms is a very long way away, probably too far away to save the forests. It could be brought much closer by government financing; the need is much more pressing than even defence budgets and space research programs, but is unlikely to be a vote-catcher. The profit motive should be sufficient incentive, but the economic returns are probably too far away. However, the outlook may change when the sea levels begin to rise, and governments will then be forced to take notice because of the enormous costs involved. Recycling carbon dioxide and preserving the forests will then be at a premium, and will perhaps usher in the new age. Are we going to continue to be reactive, only taking action as each crisis appears, letting the forests and natural ecosystems decline, the greenhouse effect develop and the necessary research only take place according to market forces? Or are we going to be proactive, undertaking the necessary research and development in time to reduce the number of world disasters, and incidentally give us some purpose in our efforts to save what is left of the last 66 million years of evolution?

I boarded the ferry and looked back longingly at Rottnest. It was back to the telephone, cars, and piles of bills. I glanced down in the water to see the shredded remains of the jellyfish stirred up in the wash. Perhaps we will not make it after all. Evolution usually has many tries before it succeeds in any new advance. After our demise, the world may be overtaken by the rodents and perhaps they will be in the same predicament in another 65 million years time, wondering what it was that led to the extinction of the human race. Or would it be the ants?...

Index

Numbers in italic are illustrations

Abalones, 92
Aboriginal, 13, 15, 17, 19, 23, 26–7, 30, 35, 40–2, 47, 67, 70–1, 85, 106, 108, 172
Acanthocarpus, 171
Acclimatisation Societies, 13
Accountability, 57
Acid rain, 18, 117, 140
Adelaide, 16
Africa, 72
Agriculture, 16, 18, 51, 84, 97, 146
Agriculturalists, 80
Agricultural land, 128
AIDS, 57, 172
Air pollution, 18, 24, 26, 117
Albany whaling, 122
Albatross, 122
Algae, 93–4, 106, 148
Algal blooms, 154
Alga culture, 94, 121
   farms, 134
   power, 95
Aluminium, 140
America, 39
Ammonite, 20
Animals, 149
Animal proteins, 158
Ant orchid, 54
Antarctica, 38, 72, 92, 118, 144

Ants, 35, 73–4, 79, 95, 106, 173, 174
Aphids, 19, 71
Araucaria, 19
Architecture, 24
Argentine ant, 16
Aridity, 107
Atmosphere, 20, 85, 116–17, 146
Aurora, 141
Avocets, *161*

Baboon flower, 25
Bacillus cereus, 60
Bacteria, 35, 60–1, 94–5, 117, 158
Bacterial culture, 158
Bandicoots, 17, 49, 70, 84
Banjine, *32*
Banjo frog, 52
Bankers, 56
Banksia, 20, 36, 84, *88–9, 102*
Bardie grubs, 41–4
Basalt, *138*, 143–4
Bassendean sands, 24
Bates, Daisy, 23
Bauxite, 28, 160
Beech, 19, 20, 26, 30, 120, 128, 140
Bees, 27
Bettong, *25*, 145
Bilby, 17
Biological warfare, 152

Bio-engineering, 95, 121
Bird observatory, 72, *75*, 80
Birds, 80
Birth control, 56
Blackbird, 13
Blackberries, 13
Blackboy, *9*, 14, 15, *156*
Blackbuck, 14
Black point, 143
Bladderwort, 38
Blowfish, 23
Blowflies, 150–1
Blowfly, 151
Blue-lady orchid, 28
Bluebottle, 92
Bluebush, 68
Blue-tongue, 107
Bluff knoll, *111*
Bobtail, 26–7
Boddington, 38, 59
Boodies, 47
Borneo, 129
Bottlebrush, *111*
Botulism, 154
Bourke parrot, 82
Box poison, 49
Boyagin, 48–9
Bracken, 130
Brazil, 85
Brine shrimps, 161
Bristlebirds, 17
Bronze Age, 50, 82
Brown, 82

Brush wallaby, *36*, 49
Bulldog ants, 73, *74*
Bullich, 129
Bunbury basalt, 143
Bunny orchid, *115*
Butterflies, 13–14, 108
Butterfly orchid, *115*

Cacti, 68
Calla lilies, *156*
Callitris, 19, 54
CALM, 133
Caltrop, 58
Camels, 72
Canadian fleabane, 13
Canetoad, 17
Canna lilies, 24
Cape arid, *88*
Cape tulips, 25
Capeweed, 24–5
Carbon Dioxide, 18, 20, 27, 59, 61, 94, 105–6, 117–19, 146, 174
Carboniferous, 153
Carotenoids, 94
Castes, 173
Caterpillars, 74
Cats, 47
Cats, native, 17
Cattle, 59, 72
Causeway, 25
Cave deposits, 72
Caves, 70, 145
Cedar, *135*, 139

Cellulose, 158
CFC, 106
Chalk, 20
Chimpanzees, 158
Chittick, *109*
Chlorine, 106
Christmas tree, 42, *43*, 83
Clearance, 47
Clear felling, 131
Clematis, 128
Cliff, 73, 81, 103
Climate, 93, 119, 146
Clones, 173
Coal, 20, 38, 103
Cockatoo, black, *40*, 47, 82, *87*
Cockatoos, Major Mitchell, *76*
Cocklebiddy, 70
Collie, 20, 38–9
Colonialism, 67
Comet, 20, 67
Companies, 56
Complexity, 173
Conservation, 104, 133–4
Coppice, 35
Coppicing, 132
Coral reefs, 163
Cormorants, 152
Corncockle, 91
Corridors, 86
Cowfish, *90*
Cowslip orchid, 28
Crabbing, 152
Crabs, 162
Cranes, 105, 108
Cranefly, 139
Crayfish, 140
Cretaceous, 20, 23, 72, 81, 143–4
Crimson chat, 69, *77*
Crows, 16, 82, 84
Cyanobacteria, 93–4, 116, 148
Cyclone, 52
Cypress, 54

Damselfly, *139*, 140
Darling fault, 20, 26, 144
Darling scarp, 20, 24
Darters, 152, *154*
Dating, 23
Deer, 13
Deer park, 29
D'Entrecasteaux, 86
Diamonds, 55
Dibbler, 96
Dictionaries, 162
Dieback, jarrah, *34*, 36, 40, 107
Dieback, rural, 18
Diet, 80
Dingoes, 49, 70–1
Dinosaurs, 20, 56, 72, 153
Diprotodons, 58, 72, 131, 145, 150
Disease, 172
Distributions, 170
DNA, 61, 79, 130
Dogs, 72
Dogs, domestic, 70
Dolphins, 160, 169
Domestic animals, 79, 149
Domesticated, 80
Domestication, 91, 93
Donkey orchid, 28
Donkeys, 72
Doublegees, 58
Doves, 16
Downland, 28, 47
Dragonfly, *140, 153*, 154, *155*, 157, 158
Drakensberg Mts, 40, 144
Drought, 92
Drought relief, 51
Dryandra, 48–9
Dugite, 164
Dunnart, *125*
Dustbowl, 52
Dwellingup, 29

Eagle, 84
Earthworms, 106

Echidnas, 145
Ecology, 20, 171
Education, 56
El Nino, 92
Eland, 14
Elbow orchid, 27, *32*, 109
Ellen brook, 23
Elm, 30
Elm disease, 18
Emu, 37
Enchanted forst, *138*
Enclosure Acts, 41
Eocene, 72
Erosion, 50–1, 53, 56, 104
Eucalypts, 62
European disease, 172
European wasps, 68
Evolution, 79, 149
Evolution, social, 74
Exotic species, 170
Experiments, 170
Extinction, 30, 37, 145
Extinction, mass, 69, 70, 71
Extinctions, 20
Eyre, 69, 86, 122

Factory farming, 158
Famine, 56–7
Farmers, 52, 56, 84, 105
Farming, 62, 105, 158
Farmland, abandoned, 104
Fashion, 58
Fauna, soil, 106
Feldspars, 61
Fence lines, 71
Fertiliser, 16, 18, 152, 154
Finance houses, 56
Fire, 15, 17, 18, *21*, 26, 29, 36, 37, 41, 71, 97, 108–9, 128
Fire tail finch, 17, 107
Fish, 95, 154, 160
Fish hook bay, *167*
Fisheries, 56, 132
Fishing, 127, 152
Flies, 139
Flinders, Matthew, 82, 86
Flood, 52, 146
Fluorine, 27
Fluoroacetic acid, 27
Fluoroacetate, 49
Flying fish, 160
Forestry, 16, 29, 47, 131–2, 152
Forestry Commission, 30, 50, 91, 132–3
Forest law, 29
Forest products, 58
Forests department, 133
Forrest, John, 13
Fossil, 20, *22*, 163
Fossil fuel, 56, 67
Fox, 13, 16, 27, 37, 47–8, 71–2, 97, 164
Frazer, 23
Freesias, 17
Fremantle, 23
Fresh water, 94
Fritillary, 14
Frog, 52, 115, 120, *123*
Frog, Banjo, *46*
Frog, Spotted, 55
Fungi, 35, 79, 94, 95

Galahs, 16–17, 47
Garnet, 103
Gas production, 94
Genesis, 23
Genetic codes, 150
Genetic diversity, 14
Genetic engineering, 94, 149, 150–1, 173
Genetic fingerprinting, 170
Genetic variation, 120
Geneticists, 170
Geology, 23
Geraldton, 20
Giant kangaroos, 72
Gibbons, 25
Gidgegannup, 28, 36
Gilgies, 23

Gingin, 20
Glaciation, 24
Glacial, 35
Gladioli, *12*, 17
Global habitat, 56
Glossopteris, 39
Gnats, 115
Goanna, 27
Goats, 59, 72
Gold, 38, 55, 58–62, 67
Goldfinches, 13
Gondwanaland, 26, 140, 144
Gould, 17
Granite, 52, 83, 86
Grasses, 16, 150
Grazing, 30, 35, 42, 58–9
Great Mammals, 72
Greenfly, 19
Greenhouse effect, 20, 52, 61, 85–6, 92, 95, 106, 134, 146, 163
Greenland, 118
Green revolution, 150–1, 157, 172
Greenstone, 59–60
Grevillea, 54, *63*
Ground parrot, 96
Guildford, 24
Gulls, 91
Gum trees, *65*
Gungurru, *45*
Gypsum, 67

Habitat destruction, 56
Habitat recognition, 25
Hakea, *64*, 109
Hare wallabies, 145
Harvest mouse, 91
Heaths, 20, *44*, 50, 82, 146
Heirisson, 23
Helmet orchid, *112*, 115
Henge-like, 128
Hesperantha, 25
Himalayas, 62
Honeybees, 14
Honeyeaters, 14, 54, 82, 86, *89, 91*
Honey-possum, 84, *91*, 146
Horses, 25, 72, 80
House mice, 97
Human populations, 164
Human society, 173
Hydrogen, 94

Ice Ages, 28, 30, 38, 51, 58, 69, 72, 82, 118–19, 142, 145–7
Ice caps, 70, 118, 146
Ice sheet, 92
Ilmenite, 143
Immunity, 172
India, 26, 144
Indians, red, 40
Infra-red, 27
Insecticides, 16, 154
Insectivorous plants, 15
Insects, 18
Intelligence, 79
Intelligence, super, 174
Invertebrates, 127
Iron ore, 67
Island, 83
Island ecology, 171
IVF program, 173
Ivory, 57

Jargon, 162
Jarrah, 20, 28–30, *33*, 35–6, 40, 129
Jellyfish, 92, 173
Jurassic, 20

Kalbarri, *22*
Kalgoorlie, *65*
Kangaroo, *11*, 17, 35, 37, 41, 49, 58, 91, *112*, 164
Kangaroo paw, *11*, 13, 83
Kanowna, 60
Karri forest, 120, *126*, 128–9, 131, *138*, 139, 145–6

Keratin, 158
Kestrel, *160*, 162
Kidney iron ore, 116, *121*
Kingia, 83
Kings Park, *10*, 13–16, 18, 19, *21*, 23, 50, 86
Kinnear, Jack, 48
Koalas, 131, 145
Kurrajong, 17

Lake George, 41
Lakes, salt, 105
Lamprophyres, 60
Land degradation, 56
Language, 162
Larks, 13
Laterite, 27
Lava, 61, *138*
Leaf miners, jarrah, 36, 170
Lechenaultia, *102*
Leeuwin block, 144
Legumes, 36
Lemming, 55–6, 95
Leptomeria, 54
Levillain, 23
Library, 67, 158, 160
Lichen, *45*
Lightning, 71
Limestones, 20, 24, 72, 119, 145, 148, 161
Livistona, 19
Logging, 129, 160
Lorikeets, 83, *85*, 86, 130
Lucky Bay, *90*
Lupins, 80

Macrozamia, 35, 41
Magpies, 84
Major Mitchell, *76*, 81
Malaria, 153
Malleefowl, 17, 72–3, *78*
Mallee, 98
Malthus, 93
Mammals, 72
Mammon, 85
Mammoth cave, 145
Mangles, Ellen, 13
Mangrove, 148
March fly, 86, *91*, 150, *151*
Marine life, 169
Marri, 36, 129
Marron, *137*, 139–41
Mars, 119
Mayfly, 140
Meat-ants, 79
Meckering, 59
Megornithids, 72
Merino, 158
Mesolithic, 30
Methane, 27, 60–1, 94, 117–19
Methane hydrate, 60
Mica, 103
Midas, 55, 57
Midges, 115, 154
Milankovic model, 118
Mineral sands, 142
Mining, 28, 62, 96–7, 160
Miocene, 72, 150
Mistletoe, *44*
Mitochondria, 130
Mole, golden, 17
Monazite, 143
Moort gum, 109
Mosquito orchid, 115
Mosquitoes, 151, 153–4
Motorways, 91
Mottlecah, 54
Mountain bell, 107, *114*
Mountain ducks, *166*
Mt Arid, *87*
Mt Barren, *100*
Mt Hassell, *113*
Mt Trio, *113*
Multinational companies, 56
Mycorrhizal, 35, 37
Myxomatosis, 30, 57

Napoleonic wars, 132
Narrows, 18
National parks, 98
Natural selection, 80, 120, 158

Neolithic, 30, 42, 48, 50, 79, 82, 93, 119, 128, 130-1, 133
Neolithic extermination, 120
New forest, 29, 98
Nickel, 61-2
Nightjar, 54
Nitrogen, 35, 152
Noah, 146
Nodulated, 150
Nodularia, 152
Noisy scrub bird, 96, 108
Nothomyrmecia, 73
Nuclear science, 151
Nuclear winter, 20
Nullarbor, 68
Numbat, *48*, 49, 70
Nutrients, 16

Oak, 30, 132
Oak wilt, 18
Obsolescence, 58
Ocean fisheries, 56
Oceans, 85
Octopus, 169
Oil, 60, 62, 67
Oldfields, 51, 104-5
Orbit, earth's, 118
Orchids, 130
Ord river, 103
Organisations, social, 74
Osprey, *168*, 171
Ostriches, 14
Oxygen, 94, 116-17
Ozone, 106, 117

Paper, 57-8, 94, 134
Pasqueflower, 91
Pastoral industry, 16, 62
Pastoral land, *66*
Pastoralists, 71
Paterson's curse, *22*, 24-5
Pea, Bitter, *31*
Peat, 119
Pelican, *6*, 23, 152
Pemberton, 129
Peppermint Grove, 19
Permian, 20, 26, 38, 70, 139
Persoonia, 35
Perup, 37
Pesticides, 16, 151, 162
Petrels, 122
Pharmaceuticals, 121
Pheasants, 13
Phosphate poisoning, 42
Phosphorus, 35, 152
Photosynthesis, 94, 149
Pigface, 69, *77*
Pillow-lava, 61
Pine, 40, 82
Pink Lake, 93
Pitcher plant, 129
Plastics, 94
Poison, 49
Pollen, 14
Pollination, 14-15, 27, 84
Pollution, air, 18, 24, 26, 117
Population, 55, 57, 134, 164, 169, 172-2
Populations, human, 93
Porongurups, *114*
Possums, 49, 91
Post-Neolithic, 93, 121, 158, 173-4
Potoroo, *96*, 97, 145
Poverty, 56
Prawns, 95
Predator, 72, 154, 164, 171
Pre-Cambrian, 23
Prehistory, 145

Prescribed burning, 35
Prickly moses, 36
Primroses, 25, 30
Privatisation, 134
Prospecting, 28
Proterozoic, 60
Proteins, 158
Pterosaur, 122, 153
Pygmy possum, *34*

Qualup bell, 107
Quarantine, 68
Quartz, 54, 59, *66*, 142
Quartzite, 103
Queensland fruit fly, 68
Quokka, 37, 161, 164, *166*, 169, 171-2
Quondong, 54, *65*

Rabbit, 13, 42, 47, 49, *71*, 80, 97, 133
Radiata pine, *167*, 171
Radioactive, 143
Radiocarbon, 145
Rainfall, 53, 128
Rare earths, 143
Rare species, 157
Ravens, 16, *82*
Recherche Archipelago, 87
Red flowering gum, *123*, 127-8
Regent parrot, 82
Research, 127, 151
Reservoirs, 37
Reserves, 93
Revegetation, 134
Rhino, 58
Rift valleys, 26
Ripple marks, 116
Robin, 13, 36
Robin hood, 29
Rock crabs, 170
Rock lobsters, 163
Rock wallaby, 48-9, 83, 145-6
Rocks, age, 23
Rodents, 174
Roe, Septimus, 13, 103
Roes Rock, 103
Romans, 30
Roman culture, 158
Root nodules, 150
Roots, 29, 35
Rossiter, Captain, 86, 122
Rottnest Island, 18, 25, *165*
Royal hakea, 96, *99*, 103, 107, 109
Rutile, 143

Salination, 42
Salmon gum, 42, *43*
Salmon Point, *165*
Salmonella, 172
Salt, 38, *46*, 51, 53, 56, 67, 120, 161
Saltbushes, 68
Sand dunes, *73*, *75*, 80, 142, 144
Sandalwood, 54
Sawpite, 17
Scarlet pimpernel, 13
Scarlet runner, 27
Scented orchid, *32*
Science, 151
Scorpion fly, *38*, 39, 139
Scott river, 143
Sea level, 70, 92, 146, 163, 174
Sea eagle, 92
Sea scorpion, *22*
Seed eating, 109
Seismic lines, 62

Sexual reproduction, 149
Sharks, 127
Sheep, 59, 72, *88*
Sheep farming, 158
She-oaks, 24, 35
Sherwood forest, 29
Sibelius, 131
Skeleton weed, 68
Slavery, 79
Slipper orchid, 109
Smog, 26
Smokers, 61
Snails, 120
Snapper, 23
Social evolution, 74, 79
Social relationships, 169
Society, 79, 173
Soil, 15-16, 18, 35, 50-1, 97, 104-6, 132
Soil erosion, 56
Solar energy, 121
Solar power, 67, 94
Solar wind, 141
Sound, 154
Soursob, 25
South Africa, 17, 25
Southern Cross, 54
Sow-thistle, 13
Sparrows, 16, 68
Spears, 17
Species, 28
Speciation, 28
Spiders, 18-19, 47, 119, 128, 153, 158
Spinebills, 14
Spirula, *170*, 171
Spongelite, 103
Spongelite cliffs, *101*
Sponges, 103
Squids, 160
Starfish, 169
Starlings, 16, 68, 81
Stilt, *154*, 161
Stinging nettles, 171
Stirling, Captain, 13, 23-4
Stirlings, *111*
Stock market, 57
Stone-Age, 30
Stonehenge, 128
Stromatolites, 60, 117, 148-9, 152, *155*
Stumps, 29
Sturt pea, 27, *76*
Sugar cane, 58, 134
Sundew, *10*, 15
Sunfish, 92
Sunspot, 141-2, 147
Superphosphate, 18
Super-intelligence, 174
Super-societies, 79
Surrey, 13, 20
Swamp bottlebrush, 127, *137*
Swan, *8*, 23, 152
Swan river, 18-19, 23-4
Swan Valley, 24
Symbiosis, 35, 149

Talc, 61
Tammar wallaby, 83, *95*, 164
Tanyderid, 139
Tar pits, 145
Technology, 159, 173
Tektites, 67
Temperature, 53, 117-19
Termites, 54, 74, 79, 106
Tertiary, 119, 128, 144
Textiles, 158
Thorium, 143
Thylacine, 70, 131, 145, 164
Thylacoleo, 72

Tiger snake, 164
Timescale, 23
Tingle trees, 128
Titanium, 143
Toad, cane, 17
Toolbrunup, *112*, *113*
Tourism, 42, 98
Tourists, 131
Toxic sprays, 18
Trap, 80
Tree farming, 30
Triassic, 30
Trigger plants, 128, *130*
Tropical rainforest, 56, 120
Truffles, 37
Tuart, 17, 164
Tuna, 127
Tutanning, 48-9
Two Peoples Bay, 107

Ultraviolet, 27, 106, 117
Understorey, 29
Uranium, 67

Valley of the Giants, *124*
Value, monetary, 84
Vandals, 158
Vegetables, 94, 157
Veldt grass, 17
Velvet ant, 73
Venus, 64, 117, 119
Vineyards, 24
Virus, 153
Vlamingh, 19, 26

Wagtails, yellow, 81
Wallabies, 17
Warren River, *136*, 139
Wasp, 14, 109, 173
Wasp, European, *68*
Waste products, 34
Watercress, 24
Water quality, 153
Water rat, 140
Watsonias, 17, 25
Wattle-bird, 9, 14
Wattles, 35
Wave Rock, 52, *53*
Weather, 70, 93
Weedkiller, 16
Weeds, 16, 25, 47, 51
Whales, 58, 122, 127, 160
Whaling, 122, 132
Wheat-belt, 42, *44*, 50, 52
Whipbirds, 17, 96
White-fronted chat, 69, 161
Wild oats, 150
Wildlife management, 133
Wildwood, 30, 41
William the Conqueror, 29, 98, 133
Willy wagtail, 16, 18
Winkles, 169-70
Wombats, 81, 145
Woodchip, 30, 134, 148
Wookey Hole, 145
Wool, 58
World population, 172
Woylie, *25*, 37, 47-9, 71, 164
Wrens, 36

Yabbie, 140
Yams, 41
Yates, 109
Year, 117
Yellowdine, 54
Yilgarn Block, 59, 116, 144

Zircon, 143